Everything
and More...

Randi McKinnon

Inks and Bindings
888-290-5218
www.inksandbindings.com
orders@inksandbindings.com

Table of Contents

Chapter 1

I sit here looking out over my backyard watching flies buzzing about, I try to catch a little warmth from the last rays of the setting sun. Every time a small gust of a fading breeze rustles through the branches of the lovely birch trees, the leaves drift ever so gracefully, landing softly on the cedar deck reminding me of big yellow snowflakes.

The blackbirds, sparrows, and wild finches share their food at the feeder and occasionally a squabble breaks out, and it ends as quickly as it starts. I really love to sit out on the deck and take in all of nature. When I smell the flower fragrances mixed with the fruit fragrances, I'm thankful for my hay fever medication that lets me enjoy such beauty. While my eyes take this all in, my memory takes me back to a different fall, long ago, and I think of the individual turns my life has taken since then.

It all started in a small community in Northern Norway. My birthplace is a picturesque village surrounded by tall, jagged mountains with small green meadows at their feet. Dotted through the scenery are houses and barns painted bright reds, blues, and yellows. Between the houses runs an unpaved road carved out of the mountainside, looking like a snake making its way out of the village and on to the next village 5 km away. Since Fiskfjord (which means fish fiord) lies at the end of a big and long sea inlet and is very deep a lot of fish swim deep there at different times of the year. This place is for some, the only income from fish that they have. Many of the children learn to handle a rowboat by the time they are 6 to 7 years old. I learned it when I was 10 years old. My father was my hero and the most wonderful man in my young life. He stood 5ft. 11 inches had a husky build and blue-grey eyes that looked stern when he wasn't smiling. When he did smile, his eyes lit up and he showed a row of pearly whites. I loved him and in my young eyes, he could do no wrong.

When the war broke out, my father enlisted. He fought at the front for a while, then he was transferred to one of the main headquarters in a town in the northern part of the country. Once, while talking to one of his superiors, he mentioned that he would like to make the Army his career and learn a trade. The superior asked my father what he liked to do best. He replied that next to fishing, he liked cooking the best. He was then transferred to the main kitchen as an apprentice, and a year later, he became the chef when the main chef was transferred to another regiment. I always enjoyed it when Mama allowed me to travel to visit him. I traveled by ferry boat which took 5 hours and was under the watchful eyes of the captain since I was only 7 years of age. And had to be in the wheelhouse most of the time until I was handed to Papa. I'd run across the gangway and Papa would twirl me and tell me he loved me and had missed me a lot. I loved riding in the Army truck because while he drove, let me stand up in the cab and I could watch traffic. My visit usually went too fast, I thought. During the day while Papa worked, I would sneak in to see him, he would give me a hug and send me on my way out of the kitchen. I also visited with some of the men, who were Papa's friends or play. Other men had their wives visiting and they would bring their children. I was never bored there!

All too soon the trip would end and it was time to return home again! I lived for those rare occasions when Papa would come home on leave. While he was home, I wouldn't leave his side and he seemingly didn't mind! Mama would be a little jealous but I didn't realize this until years later, when I grew up and reflected back on it.

Mama and Papa married young, Papa was 20 years and Mama was 18 years. A year before my birth, they had a son, by the name of Jon Arvid and he died of sudden infant death syndrome at 5 weeks old.

One year later Mama was with child and that was me. I got all the love and attention for two and was spoiled a lot! I quickly became 'the apple of my father's eye' and he refused me nothing. At the same time, Mama taught me obedience. I soon knew exactly how far I could 'stretch' it before I got into trouble!

Mama would reprimand me more often than Papa would. Between 7 and 10 years old, I had the usual illnesses associated with children, the cold influenza. When I was 9 years old, I developed an infection in my right ear serious enough to send me to the hospital.

I didn't know until later that Papa was also at the hospital on the floor above me and he got the information that he had inoperable testicular cancer or ITC as it was called. He had been injured while working at the army base, helping move gasoline drums by trucks from a sunny spot into a cool mountain cave, when he slipped and landed with one leg on each side of the truck bed. He said he was alright week after week but he was in constant pain. Finally, he saw the doctor, who put him in the hospital right away. Two weeks after I came home from the hospital, Papa came home too.

All our bedrooms were upstairs but Papa was too weak and was unable to walk upstairs and Mama made the living room couch into a permanent bed for him. To my many questions, Mama cut short by saying that Papa had gotten injured and had to stay home with us until he got better. I was so very happy that I could be close to him all the time now that I promised myself that I would play as little as possible with my friends so I could sit and hold his hand and tell him about my day. His hands would get so cold and I wondered why and Papa would say, "I'm just not getting enough exercise."

After Papa had been home for six weeks, I began to wonder why he didn't get up and walk. When I asked him why not, he'd squeeze my hand and look away, and out of my respect and love for him and

3

Mama's warning not to tire him out, I kept quiet. The days and weeks went by and Papa grew more and more tired. One day after Papa had been home two months, Mama would not let me in to visit with him. I got very upset and ran outside crying. To this day I don't know why but I started eating 'dirt'! Something was very wrong, and I thought that if I only could hold his hand, all my questions about him would be answered. My tears blended with the dirt and I must have looked terrible, but I felt totally numb and I didn't know why! After a while, Mama came looking for me. In her usual calm voice, she asked me to come in and she'd help me so I could ride my bicycle to my grandmother's house and give a note to my oldest uncle, (this was Papa's family). Papa had three brothers, two younger and one older. The oldest brother was 36 years old at that time and two months before, he had become a Christian and much later I understood why Mama wanted my uncle there at Papa's bedside.

My uncle and I rode on my bike back to my home and when we arrived, he went straight to Papa's bedside. A short while later, he came out crying. I knew Papa had passed away.

Something snapped within me and I ran into the house while thoughts raced through my mind. The only thought that stayed was that if Papa didn't live, then neither would I. I grabbed one of Papa's razor blades, but at that second, I felt a pair of strong arms grabbing me from behind.

I screamed, "Let me go, I'm going with him", over and over again but my uncle held me tight, hugging and rocking slowly side to side while I cried and screamed and he cried as well. I don't know how long we stood there but after a while, he released his grip and gently took the razor blade from my hand and felt numb all over and suddenly I began to vomit. There I stood, vomit running down my front, onto my shoes and the floor. I looked down and saw that my vomit was black from the dirt I had eaten earlier and now I was covered with black, earth-smelling vomit but I didn't care what I looked or smelled like! My uncle picked me up in his arms and carried me to the creek behind our house.

"Let me help you get cleaned up, he said as he took his handkerchief from his pocket, dipped it in the water, and started wiping my dress. While he wiped, he kept talking to me, but I didn't hear a word of what he was saying, no sounds came through, even though I watched his lips moving. I looked past him and saw the creek's water tumbling over the rocks which was a sound I always enjoyed listening to when I played with my doll by the creek for hours at a time, but not on this day. Everything was silent, even the birds I saw flitting from tree to tree and I kept wondering why I couldn't hear them or anything else! After he washed my dress and shoes off, he stuck my feet in the creek and washed them too and the water really felt warm to me. Then he carried me inside and set me on the kitchen table. Mama walked in to change my clothes and her eyes were red from crying. My eyes searched her face for a little smile she always had for me but I found none and I was angry with her. I wanted to yell and scream and kick her for not caring for me enough to tell me everything was alright and that we would make it, but I couldn't find the strength to speak!

I felt hot tears running down my face and Mama saw them and quickly wiped them, kissed my cheek, and stroked my hair but I didn't get the hug my body was screaming for from her. Mama spoke to my uncle and said something and he nodded and smiled. He reached out his hand toward me as he said; "Come let's go!" "Go where?" I got my voice back. He said," We were riding my bike back to Grandma's house because I was to stay with her for a few days!" That was my favorite place to be, where I could be with the animals and talk with them. We rode back to Grandma's and my uncle told her about Papa's passing away. For a while, Grandma stood with her back to me and facing the window and her shoulders were shaking. With tears flowing they turned toward me and said;" You poor child!" She encircled her arms around me and rocked me gently. I started crying again, but this time not from despair. It was more of a release of sadness for the loss of the person that I loved the most in my whole world. I realized that I would not see him again until I entered the Heavenly gates, Grandma said.

Sitting there on Grandma's lap with her two strong arms around me so gently yet so secure, I began to relax for the first time in many hours. "Where did uncle go?" I asked her. "He and your other two uncles have gone to help your Mama, she's going to need a lot of help for a while," she said all the while humming a tune and I leaned against her chest and eventually I fell asleep. Several days passed but I still wasn't going home and didn't even think of my home and Mama. Grandma was quiet-spoken but stern. A lady who always wore black stockings with black shoes, a gray dress with a white apron. Her hair was gray and very thick and had a blunt haircut just above the shoulders. My Grandma was no stranger to hard work. After Grandpa died of stomach cancer, she raised 3 sons by herself, while working the farm and tended to goats, sheep, chickens, and a cow named Star that had a patch of white fur on her forehead in the shape of a star, hence her name.

All the animals knew me on sight and Star would 'moo' softly, perk her ears, and stand waiting for me to come and put my arms around her neck and give her a hug. Oh yes- I told Star lots of secrets as she stood chewing her cud. Sometimes she would even put her head on my shoulder and burp in my ear and I didn't care much for that and I told her how rude it was.

Every morning after milking, Grandma would let them out of the barn and let me 'herd' them up towards the hills to a grazing area, about a 20-minute walk from the house. There I would leave them to graze until 5 PM when they would come from the grazing field to the fence to be let in for milking and retiring to the barn for the night. Grandma made cheese and butter from both the goats and cows and sold the cheese and most of the eggs. Her little farm was perched on the side of a hill among huge boulders as anybody else, they all had to make do with what they could get from that good and giving soil. I had been at the farm one week when one morning Grandma cleared her throat and said, "Today your Papa is to be buried. It may be a good

6

idea for you to go home. Your Mama will need all the help and support you can give her!" Suddenly I felt a tug of guilt because I had not given Mama one single thought while staying with Grandma, it was as if she didn't exist and Papa's death was just a bad dream. Now I started thinking about what Mama had gone through all alone for the last few days, and then I knew what I had to do! We finished breakfast in silence, then I helped Grandma clear the table. I gave her a big kiss and hug and thanked her for letting me stay there. When I climbed on my bike, Grandma and my uncles asked me to tell Mama that they would be right along to attend the funeral. While I rode home, I had a lot to think about what home would be without Papa, without that piece in

My puzzle of the future!

Mama was sitting at the kitchen table when I walked in the door.

A little lady just 4 ft-8 in, slightly plump with black hair and clear blue eyes that sparkled when she smiled. Today, the eyes did not sparkle. She turned toward me as I opened the door and opened her arms and I ran to her. Mama rocked me gently and repeated my name over and over, her voice growing fainter each time. I looked up at her face and saw tears in her eyes that rolled down her cheeks. After a while, she pulled a chair from under the table and motioned to me to sit down. Blowing her nose, she asked if I wanted to talk and I nodded.

"While we talk would you have a cup of coffee?" she asked. She seldom let me drink coffee but when she did, she taught me to hold a lump of sugar in my mouth, then sip the brew through the sugar lump. I liked coffee like that! She fixed a cup for me and one for herself, then she lit a cigarette and taught for a moment.

"We need to make plans for the future, you and I," she said finally. We talked, I don't know how much time passed, and then there was a knock on the door.

"Come in," Mama said.

The door opened and an older lady walked in dressed all in black- black coat, black dress with small white dots, black shoes, and stockings. Mama jumped up and embraced the woman, and they both cried, then Mama turned to me and said;" Come and shake hands with your Grandma Kristine!" It was Mama's mother. At first, Grandma shook my hand and I curtsied, then she quickly wiped a tear from her eye and said; "Let's not be that formal." She took me in her arms and gave me a hug and a kiss.

Grandma Kristine had a stern face with the same clear eyes as Mama that twinkled when she smiled. Her dark hair was flecked with strands of gray and pulled back in a large bun. She took charge of the food preparation. Some of the neighbors came to help as well, which was customary at every funeral or any other get-together in Norway in those days and may still be, I do not know. After a while, the people started arriving, and the door to the living room was finally unlocked and opened. I got to see Papa one last time as he lay in the casket all dressed in white. He looked so peaceful in that long gown with his hands folded in prayer that I hoped he'd open his eyes and give me his special wink, but deep down, I knew he never would again! Since Papa's death, I had not been left alone for a second. So, after all the neighbors arrived and were standing around talking, drinking coffee, and eating food, I decided to take a walk into the woods where Papa and I used to explore. Without telling anybody where I was going, I took off, walking and walking, all the time pretending Papa was at my side, maybe he was, in spirit, but it sure felt as if he were there. My home was built on a small plateau with a road about 500 feet above the house. Below the house, was a hillside that sloped down toward the sea in stair steps. Above the road was another large hillside dotted with huge boulders, caves, and trees. The ground produces lingonberries, wild blueberries and a few other berries not known in this country.

I noticed the berries were not ripe and remarked to Papa that' it 'wouldn't be long now before they could be picked'. Then I heard a loud whistle and somebody calling my name frantically. It was all three of my uncles who were trying to find me. I answered their call and headed home. When I got there, mama said I had missed the small service the pastor had given before we left for the graveyard.

Chapter 2

She checked me over to see if I was clean enough as I had my Sunday best on. Since there were only two cars in the whole village and they were ¾ ton trucks, the procession used horse-drawn wagons. We had 6 kilometers traveling to the graveyard. All the people stood around the casket and once again, I got that numb feeling that I could not understand what was happening to my body. The pastor stood at the head of the casket and he looked like a kind of grandfather who would sit and tell stories and laugh out loud! I looked at the people standing around the casket and how sad they looked some were crying and I wanted to cry but I had no tears left. I stood between Mama and Papa's mother and on Mama's other side stood Mama's mother and she was looking at me. She looks just like a 'farm woman' should look, tall, strong, and a bit overweight. In Norway, people used to say 'If a woman isn't overweight, she probably doesn't know how to cook'! But there my Grandma stood, with a straight back and her eyes lowered in respect of Mama's sorrow. I hardly knew her but ever since she had been living with us, I had come to respect her tremendously. She had a farm that she sold to come and live with or close to Mama to help her in her time of need. Mama needed help because she was what the doctors called handicapped. She was born with both hip sockets on the outside of the hip and the doctors put her in traction for two years from ages 4 to 6, I think I was told. Grandpa left Grandma for a younger woman close to Mama's age whom she later married. But Grandma raised Mama and my uncle, Mama's brother who was 2 years younger than Mama, along with her large farm. I was only 2 or 3 years old at the time and don't recall any of that. I never thought about how tired Mama would get during the day when I'd see her sitting at the table with her coffee cup and cigarette, trying to take a drag of the cigarette while yawning. Mama was a seamstress by profession and would sit and do late-night sewing for somebody. She also had 7 goats, a bunch of chickens, and a pig which would be slaughtered for Christmas feasting after Mama had prepared, canned, and pickled the pig. I strongly disliked the smell in the kitchen of the canning of pork but it sure tastes good later! Grandma helped but Mama insisted that it was 'her' house and so she had to do most of the chores! We also had a rowboat, and that chore Grandma didn't volunteer to do, which was going fishing in our 'fiord' or bay, which Mama did several times during the week. When Mama allowed, Grandma would arrange an 'all day' berry picking' day for her and myself and I loved those trips. We'd go until we were far away from the house, then we'd find a spot and pick a few blueberries. She'd unpack the sandwiches she brought and we'd eat them and fresh berries- there's nothing better than that. We'd sit for a while and she would tell me about her youth. Oh, how I loved those trips!! Her grandma, my great-great-grandmother, was a full-blooded gypsy princess from Romania who immigrated from there with her royal family. She fell in love with my great-great grandfather but since he wasn't gypsy, she had to get special permission from the clan leader and have her fiancé adopted by the clan before they could get married! They then moved from the gypsy camp to build their own place and live like the white man did which was a strange concept for my great-great-grandma! Grandma Kristine remembered how beautiful her grandma was with long black hair that reached below her knees. She would let Grandma comb her hair and she would close her eyes and while smiling, she'd hum a tune and then sing the words softly which Grandma didn't understand. When Grandma would ask what song she was singing, she said it was a love song and then she would translate the words and teach Grandma the song by repeating it time after time. This lady was also psychic and knew of certain incidents long before they happened. Great-great grandfather's farm was on an island, separated from the mainland by a narrow passage.

Every Sunday they would cross this passage in their rowboat to go to church. The passage was noted for a very strong undertow and a surge at un-clocked times. On this special Sunday, they were on their way back from church with the whole family- great-great grandma and grandpa, their children and grandchildren, rowing across. Two strong men at the oars and great-great grandma at the rear of the boat. Suddenly she whirls and stares at the sea, saying;" I'll see you all in Heaven someday!" A very large wave rose and swept her over the side of the boat. After days of searching, she was never found.

Grandma said her grandpa was never quite the same after that day. He went through the motions of daily life but the light in his eyes had died. Almost 6 months to the day, he suffered a stroke and died.

Grandma's stories would interest me so much that I wouldn't notice it was getting dark and it was time to go home. When we came home, Mama would give Grandma a gentle scolding for staying out so late, but Grandma would only wink at me and say; "We had fun didn't we?"

In 1948, when I was 11 years old, I entered a phase where I was becoming a young woman. I started menstruating and my breasts grew to the point that Mama had to sew bras as there were none small enough to be bought. Up to this time, I had been quite a 'tomboy', playing rough sports with the boys, climbing trees, scaling rocks, fighting, and ending up with a bloody nose and torn clothes! One time in particular, Gunnar, the neighbor's boy, sat with me by the little creek that ran between our homes. We played in the water, making little dams and re-routing the flow, our conversation slid onto who we liked the best among our friends. Gunnar had a 16-year-old brother Atle and I said that I liked Atle the best. Gunnar pushed me playfully and said; "You can't have him because he is my brother." I pushed him back and before I knew it, we were rolling on the ground, pulling hair and into a real fight when suddenly, I tasted blood and Gunnar said;" Your nose is bleeding!"

I ran home to Mama and she took one look at me and said; "Been fighting with Gunnar again, have you huh?"

After she cleaned me up, she suggested that I should go out and talk it out with Gunnar to restore our friendship and I did. But Mama had something else to say since I was now becoming a young woman, I should start behaving like one and act like one as well! Although I knew what she was talking about, I just didn't want to do that quite yet- in time! About 4 months after Papa died, Grandma Kristine had a stroke, which tied Mama down even more. So, the following spring, Mama decided to go on vacation, she just had to get away, she said. She put an advertisement in our national newspaper for a caregiver for Grandma and me. At that time, we had no local papers, only nationals. The first person who answered the ad was a beautiful lady, tall and slender with long black hair past her shoulders. Her eyes were fiery brownish- black and her complexion looked like ivory. Mama thought she looked like a light-skinned gypsy. Nora was her name and she told us that her husband had signed on at Spitzbergen for one year and she was looking for something to do while he was gone. Spitzbergen is a large island located in the Arctic Sea and mining is their main work. People sign contracts for no less than one year, I believe to live and work in this harsh environment. Mama liked Nora and so did I but ALL of Grandma's sixth bells went off! Mama left on her vacation to visit her father and his young wife anyway. It was early spring and I was still in school and was gone most of the day when I came home, all was quiet and seemingly all right. When Mama returned home three weeks later, I was happy to have her back and Grandma cried when she saw Mama. Nora was paid and she left on the next ferry. A couple of days later, Mama was looking for an item and discovered it was missing along with several other things. Grandma's bed sheets that Grandma had made herself, several pieces of silverware, and even a silver thimble that my great-great-grandfather had made for Mama. Grandma started telling us about the antics of Nora. She didn't physically abuse Grandma, but while I was in school, she would deny her food while Nora sat and ate in front of Grandma. Grandma was still too weak from her stroke to exercise, so she couldn't get to the food and sat all day in the rocking chair until I came home, then after making sure Nora was out of earshot, Grandma would ask me for a bite to eat. Young me, I still thought this odd but not to question anything and we shared meals every day and I told her about my day. Mama called the police who caught up with Nora who still had the stolen items in her possession. Mama found out that she had other problems as well. Before she came to us, she had not been feeling well and had seen a doctor who then ran a few tests on her. The tests were positive for Tuberculosis. With that knowledge and ignoring doctors' warnings about treatment, she came to work for us, even though she was aware of how communicable the disease was!

I guess we were lucky, neither of us came down with the illness, but when the health department found out where she had been, they ordered all of us to come there for extensive testing. Thankfully, all testing was negative. The goods she had stolen were contaminated though, and had to be purified. The health department suggested the items to laid in a sunny room and then purified naturally for six to eight weeks. Nora was found guilty and put in jail where she died of her disease.

Mama received a letter from her husband apologizing for what she did and begging our forgiveness.

Mama ran another advertisement for a caregiver. This time a young couple with a three-year-old baby girl answered. The woman loved to tease her husband by flirting with other men. She confided in Mama that her husband was very jealous by nature and she loved to tease him. Then they would make up later and all was well again. Grandma shook her head and said; "Nothing good will come from this!"

The family stayed with us for a week so we could get to know them and, my uncles came to our house often. The woman would 'hang' all over my Uncle Hardloy (the oldest) but since he had become a Christian, he didn't want any part of her teasing and told her this in front of her husband.

One evening, her husband had had enough. He threatened her life for her cruelty. It so happened that Uncle Hardloy was at our house that evening, thank goodness. It was fall and darkness settled in earlier in the evening. The man was getting violent, but Uncle Hardloy managed to get him outside so he could talk to him. Still, something snapped in the man and he began to make sounds like an angry animal, sounds I will never forget, as long as I live. I was so nervous and upset and shaking so badly that I couldn't sit still on the chair. Mama had locked all the doors and windows so the man couldn't enter back into the house, and we still could hear my uncle talking very softly to him. Sometime during the early evening, Mama asked me to go to bed and try to get some sleep. I was happy to get away from the tension downstairs and went upstairs to sleep with the couple's little girl.

I must have been sleeping a while when I felt someone shake me awake. It was Mama, asking me to get up and get dressed quickly and come down to the living room. She wanted me to slip out the window and run and ask Gunnar's parents to come. Gunnar's father was a big, husky 6 ft-plus man. His wife was wiry with a big gray hair bun on top of her head. They both carried a lot of respect around the village. I was in such a hurry and so scared that I put my dress on backward. The zipper was now in front and the big pockets were on the back. Mama lowered me out the living room window, which was on the backside of the house and I ran through the woods to Gunnar's house and banged on the door. The bedroom window opened upstairs and his Mama saw it was me and came down and opened the door. "Why are you here at this hour?" she wanted to know.

I was out of breath from running all the way uphill but glad I was safe! I gave them the message from Mama and then I started crying. Mr. and Mrs. Hansen assured me I was safe and promised to go to my house to see if they could be of help. Before they left, they put me in their bed which was still warm. They slept on straw mattresses, and I can still remember how good their bed smelled. I buried my face in their pillow and promptly went to sleep. The next thing I remember was Gunnar shaking me awake, demanding to know why I was sleeping in his parent's bed! Again, I remembered the horror from the night before and rushed to put my clothes on, this time the right way! I ran downstairs to find out if it was safe for me to return home. Mr. and Mrs. Hansen were eating breakfast.

"It's safe to go back home," Mrs. Hansen said, "but before you go let's get a hot breakfast inside you".

I remembered I hadn't eaten since dinner early yesterday afternoon and I was terribly hungry. After I ate, I curtsied and thanked her for letting me stay and feeding me breakfast.

"If you feel scared again, tell your Mama where you are, then come back here," she said and gave me a quick hug, and I promised I would.

Walking through the woods felt good with the cool air stroking my face. I came to the creek and stood there for a while; a bit scared to go in the house for fear of what I might find. Papa wasn't here to protect me or had he been maybe he had been here- that he was sent down to protect his family- yes that I believed and summed all my courage and walked in.

Mama told me that the man had calmed down after the Hansen's had been there and, in his despair, had turned to prayer. With the help of my uncle and the Hansen's, he had become a Christian during the night! He said that he would try to live with his wife and daughter but would seek divorce if it didn't work out. He was on his knees before Grandma begged her forgiveness for bringing evil into our house and Grandma forgave him. His wife started to say something mean, but Grandma ordered her to shut her mouth and not open it until she could ask his forgiveness, which to our knowledge- she never did, at least not while they were with us. They left our home and returned to their own, with the hope of staying together for a while.

When the ordeal was over, everybody's nerves were a bit ragged, and thinking our thoughts. Now, as an adult, I can imagine that Mama longed to have a man to lean on in her mind much of the time.

Late fall was here and Christmas preparations were at hand with pickling canning and baking. The baking tradition was to bake seven different cookies and seven different breads. Clean the house top to bottom, put up clean curtains, clean homemade woven rugs on the clean floors, and clean bedding. After all the baking is done, clean the oven as well. The week before the holidays, the living room door was locked and only Mama could go in and out and only she knew where the key to the door was hidden. The day before Christmas Eve, Mama and Grandma would decorate the tree and on Christmas Eve at precisely six o'clock, the door would be opened. Our pig had been slaughtered and Mama was canning and pickling and Grandma would help with the cookie making.

I was thinking how empty the house would be because this was the first Christmas without Papa my Papa! Christmas Eve came and Mama, Grandma, and I had our bath in the wooden tub, dressed in our finest clothes, and had our dinner that was special that night. The dishes were cleared off the table and washed and special tablecloths replaced the dishes on the tables with holiday decorations everywhere and the stoves had crackling fires. I started watching the road to see if I could spot anybody coming down our road, I was thinking that Santa might be arriving soon! It had shown a lot, but now it was clear and the moon cast a magic light over the countryside, making it easy to see anyone coming down the road. Mama wanted to know why I kept watching the road. With a lump in my throat, I said that I was watching for Santa. Mama made herself busy arranging cookies on a plate while mumbling something about not thinking Santa would come because he might be too busy in other parts of the world. Finally, six o'clock arrived. Mama temporarily forgot about Santa and opened the door to the living room.

The living room table was covered with a red tablecloth and a large white candle stood in the middle and was lit. Around the candle stood plates of cookies, apples, oranges, and pears along with nuts.

Our potbelly stove had a cozy fire. I just stood there and stared at the beauty I saw. The throw pillows on the couch I remembered Grandma making and this time would be the only time they could be seen. Then my eyes moved to the tree and it was the most beautiful tree I'd ever seen, but my eyes dropped to the bottom of the tree- no packages at all! I asked Mama why there were no packages this year.

"There just wasn't any leftover money this year for presents," she said and gave me a hug. Then I recalled that about a month ago, Mama had sent me to the post office to pick up a package but she had said that it was a large number of medicines for Grandma.

At that time there suddenly were heavy footsteps coming up the stairs at the front of our house.

Mama sounded as if she was irritated as she said;" Now who could that be at this time, go and see Randi!" Before I got to the door, there was a loud knock on the door.

"Go and answer the door," Mama commanded. But I refused and positioned myself behind Grandma's chair and waited until Mama opened the door and I heard a big, booming voice asking if a girl named 'Randi' lived there. Mama answered 'yes' and invited him in. Then I peeked around the chair and saw it was Santa, I could have cried with joy- but I didn't, instead, I shook like a leaf from a little fear and a lot of respect for Santa!

He sat down, saying he was tired from all that walking from house to house. Our Santa does not ride a sleigh like they portray here in the USA, they walk.

Santa asked me to come and sit on his lap and asked me to sing a verse from Santa's song (which is a special song about Santa and what he does.) With a very shaky voice, I sang. Then studying the face, I wondered if this really was Santa or just someone with a mask. Then he 'remembered' the presents he had in his bag. He begged my forgiveness for forgetting, claiming he was getting old and was forgetting things. He gave Grandma one, and one to Mama. He stirred and looked saying he knew there was one more, there just had to be for he saw it come floating into the bag.

I struggled to hold back the tears, afraid that Santa would forget me in his forgetfulness. Finally, he pulled an oblong package from the bag and handed it to me. I curtsied deeply, saying' Thank you' and sat down on the couch to wait for Santa to tell me I could open the present. After what seemed like an eternity, but was merely a few minutes, Santa gave me the go-ahead!

'I started opening carefully so as not to tear the paper as per instructions from Mama.

Nestled inside the box was the most beautiful doll I had ever seen, with eyes that closed and a lovely dress, cap, and coat that Mama had made for her. She looked so pretty so I held her and my heart sang with joy! She looked to be the same doll I had admired months before in a catalog from a big department store in Southern Norway. Santa wanted to know if I liked the doll, I answered that I did very much and gave the doll a hug and I cried.

He wanted to know where those tears came from and that I was supposed to be happy -not sad.

I told him about Papa dying and he listened carefully, then when I finished talking, he gave me a hug and said that Papa had sent the doll for me to love and it was a special present from Papa to me. Something released inside me then and it seemed as if a door had opened to let sunlight inside me and make everything seem alright again. I had finally accepted the loss of my father on Christmas Eve, one year after his death!

Santa said 'goodbye' and left.

A little later Mama made coffee and we relaxed and had coffee and cookies, which I shared with my new 'baby' which I named 'Lise-doll' who sat on my lap all evening before I went to bed, I made Lise-doll a bed on the couch where Papa used to lay, this way he would take care of her, just in case she cried during the night!

The day after Christmas (2nd Christmas day (27th), my school had their annual Christmas party. Mama had made a new outfit for the celebration which consisted of a wine-colored velvet skirt and vest and a white silk blouse with ruffles on the collar and a new pair of lacquered shoes and my first pair of silk stockings. Since my school was 6 km away, while walking to the party, we wore our snow clothing and snow shoes and carried our party clothes in our backpacks. When we came to the school, we changed clothing. I was so proud of my new clothes and kept watching the front door for signs of Mama, who before I left the house, had said that she might come. Most parents had already arrived but no sign of Mama. I was supposed to sing the Santa song in its entirety, all 6 verses acapella, the same song which I sang a verse from for Santa at my house. The program was about to start and I felt so sad because none of my family was there but then- there was a brief commotion at the front door, and in walked Mama with Grandma in her wheelchair, my other grandma, and all three of my uncles and I was proud as punch! I sang the song on stage, remembering all 6 verses, and got applause and whistles from my uncles, my friends told me later. After the stage programs were done, the big Christmas tree was pulled out from its corner and the live candles were lit and we walked around the tree, singing Christmas songs. Mama wheeled Grandma into the circle as my other Grandma joined in and Uncle Hardloy wheeled Grandma around the tree. I walked between my Grandmas holding their hands while singing Christmas songs. After all the songs were sung, Santa came and gave each of the children a small bag of candy, and the party ended with the kitchen serving hot chocolate and cookies to everybody.

We made ready for the long walk home when I was told that my family had rented a large truck and the driver and I rode home with them. Grandma Kristine sat in front of the driver while the rest of us sat on low benches in the truck bed.

When I drifted off to sleep that evening, I was happy at the way all had happened that Christmas, and I knew that Papa had a hand in it.

Spring came and turned into summer and summer into fall. During this time Grandma and Mama had been arguing more and more about small things that suffused during the day. Usually, the arguments would end up with both of them crying. I really felt bad about the situation but I didn't know what to do about it. One day Grandma said that she would like to move to a nursing home so she wouldn't tie Mama down and thought she would be happy there.

"You're only 35 years old, you're too young to be tied down this much," she said. You should be with friends, have parties and such. Mama agreed very reluctantly but I hated the idea because I loved them both and wanted them in the same place but I knew that I had nothing to say on the matter. I had to go along with what Mama decided because I knew Grandma would never get any better and in fact- I had noticed lately that she would repeat the same sentence over and over again. Grandma was moved to the only nursing home in our area at the time. To arrive there, we had to ride the ferry for 1 ½ hours across the fiord, then a 30 min. bur ride to the home. We visited her but not as often as I had liked to do. I loved my Grandma and Mama so much and hated to see them separated like this. When I asked Mama about it, she wouldn't elaborate, and claimed I was too young to understand!

Since I had stopped acting like a tomboy, much to my playmate Gunnar's irritation, and was dressing and acting like a girl, I noticed boys taking a second look when I walked by. Their looks made me feel all warm inside along with a different, new kind of feeling-like electricity running through my body. I couldn't understand this feeling at all!

Mama decided that she needed a change again and this time she wanted to move from the area altogether and that was a shock for me to leave all my friends! She advertised in the national newspapers for a housekeeping job. While she waited for answers, fall turned into winter, which brought forth my first boyfriend! He was 16 years old, stood a head taller than me, had dark blond wavy hair and blue-gray eyes, and was very thin and lanky.

At that time 1949, everything was done quite properly and yes-I got a kiss or two and I knew he was mine but I was so afraid to get teased about him by my friends because he had been in scrapes with the law a few times for breaking into houses and stealing money. Siegfrid's mother didn't want him because he was born out of wedlock and his aunt raised him but he wasn't treated well there. His cousins would continuously tease and taunt him about his problems.

To escape, Sigfrid would come to our house, where Mama would treat him right by answering his questions about life and giving him rapt attention. One day he had a question for Mama, that was more personal than most of his questions...

"Would he be allowed to go steady with Randi?"

"Yes but no funny business!" Mama replied.

Sigfrid promised there would be none. Since he had started coming to our house, a few other young people from the village started visiting as well. Mama would serve coffee and cookies or cake as we all sat around the kitchen table talking and having a good time until late in the evening. Our village was too small for movies, radio telephones, or even dances and the young people needed a place to go and just sit and talk, especially when winter came and the weather was cold and snowy.

During the week, there wasn't much socializing as we had school to attend but we made up for that on weekends. As time passed, my friends began to accept Sigfrid, and our friendship blossomed. Mama noticed the growing closeness and tried to speak with us separately and together but our friendship just grew stronger. We still managed to hide it from our friends. When spring rolled around, Sigfrid and I would steal away to be by ourselves, going on long walks to find a place to sit and talk for hours on end. But there was never EVER any 'funny' business going on. Sigfrid was a very honorable young man who didn't believe in sex before marriage as for me, the whole idea scared me silly. I just enjoyed talking with him.

In February 1950, Mama received 35 answers to her housekeeping ad in the paper. Knowing that she could keep only one, she threw them all in the air and closed her eyes. I told her when the papers settled on the floor and she went on her knees with her eyes still closed and picked one letter.

The letter was from a bachelor in East Finnmark who needed someone to take care of his home. He owned a small shipyard and had no time to housekeep his beautiful home. His letter also said that one child was no hindrance.

Mama smiled a big smile saying "This is it- Burn the rest of the letters"!

Mama sold the house to Uncle Hardloy and we knew it would be taken care of so we packed our 'things'. Mama sent a telegram to our new 'boss', informing him of our arrival in the town of Vadso.

For me, the most difficult thing to do was to say 'goodbye' to Sigfrid and Grandma. Mama and I went to see Grandma one last time before we left the area. She had had another small stroke and didn't understand that we were leaving but during our whole visit, she kept talking about her cousin coming to visit her so we knew that she didn't realize that we were leaving for good. It was very clear to us, especially Mama that Grandma had lapsed into the past. It was very hard for me to see her like that because she was my grandma and I loved her!

But Mama explained it this way; "It's easier to leave her in this state of mind. This way she doesn't understand nor will she remember that we will be gone a long time and that we will not be able to see her. But you, Randi, try to remember her as she was a few years ago."

I still had to say 'goodbye' to Sigfrid. I clung to him and cried and we promised to write to each other. When the ferry left the dock, there were only two waving good-bye, him and Uncle Hardloy.

One year almost to the day of us leaving the village, a friend who I had been corresponding regularly with told me that Sigfrid had died. It was told that he died of cancer that nobody cared to have him checked for.

Chapter 3

The ferry brought us to a small town where we caught the steamship. It was a four-day travel by steamship up the coast to Vadso, in East Finnmark. Since I was used to traveling from the days of visiting Papa at the Army camp, I took this trip in stride. The people who worked on the ship were very friendly and let me visit most of the places on board. Only the engine room and the kitchen were off-limits, but that left the dining room, all the halls and corridors, and the bridge and bow to roam. I often went to the bow to feel the bitterly cold air and the sea spray on my face. The ground was still covered with snow, which made the air twice as cold since we were following the coastline, but I loved it. Mama sat in the smoking salon, drinking coffee and working on her embroidery. I was glad when she met some ladies who were also going to Vadso; now the trip would be easier for her with someone to talk to. I wanted to be alone and give in to the memories of the times with Sigfrid. I also caught myself wondering what our new place would be like. Would I find friends fast, and would I like it there and feel at home?

We arrived in Vadso late afternoon, but it was already getting dark. A small man no more than 5 feet 3 stood by the gangplank, and when we came down, he came over to introduce himself. He was our new boss, Hemming.

A fishing boat he had rented was waiting to take us to his village, about one and a half hours across the fjord from Vadso. By now, I was so tired of traveling that I didn't care. I crawled into one of the cots along the bow below deck and went to sleep. Mama shook me awake when we arrived at the small village of Bugoynes, our new home. I looked out. The houses stood on a treeless sandspit, which didn't look very impressive to me. I immediately wanted to go home, but Mama reminded me that we had nothing to go back to, and this is where we would stay. So, I settled down and started looking around me.

I discovered I had taken an instant dislike to our boss, and I thought I knew why. I felt he was intruding into our lives, trying to take my father's place, and I hated him for it, but I decided not to talk to Mama about my thoughts for a while. I didn't think she'd understand right then. Hemming's home, however, was very pretty. It was a large house with two stories painted white with red trim. Downstairs had an outer entrance hall, a kitchen, and a large living room. In the hall, a large winding stairway led upstairs to two large bedrooms and Hemming's shipyard office.

Hemming himself was quite soft-spoken, with a strong Finnish accent, which explained his small and stocky build. Many people from Finland, northern Norway, and northern Sweden have this build, and it is believed that it helps their bodies retain the heat needed to survive in this harsh climate.

Hemming was very well-liked and respected in Bugoynes, which came in handy for me in the future.

As I began to meet new friends, I was upset to discover that the people of the village spoke two languages, Finnish and Norwegian. After all, I had been through in the last two years, I didn't need to come to a place where I couldn't understand what they were saying. My pride wouldn't let me stand around when the young people started speaking Finnish, so I went home feeling like I had landed on another planet.

Since it was early spring, and I was finishing my sixth school year here, I was glad that the teachers, a married couple close to retiring age, were from mid-Norway and thought they were a lot of fun.

By the time summer rolled around, my newfound friends decided not to speak Finnish in front of me, and I was happy. Sometimes I came home wondering about some Finnish words I had heard. Mama suggested I ask Hemming about them, and he set me straight about them. I found out the words I had heard weren't exactly nice ones. In his mild-mannered way, Hemming offered to teach me more language phrases so I could at least understand what was going on, then answer them in Norwegian, and I readily agreed.

Soon it was time for me to graduate from the seventh grade. Our teachers, Mr. and Mrs. Hov, had an apartment above the classrooms, which is quite common in Norway; many people have businesses in their homes to save on rent and to make it easier to get to work. On the day of our graduation in June 1951, Mr. and Mrs. Hov invited all 24 of us up to their apartment for hot chocolate and cookies. We were given our diplomas and a short speech about the future, along with a few pointers on life. Mr. Hov pointed out that I was the youngest student that he had helped graduate in all his years of teaching.

"Since Randi is only 14 years old, she has some fast running to do to catch up with the rest of you," he said with a smile and a wink.

His words didn't have an impact on me until I was walking home. When I thought about what he had said, I started crying.

I walked into our house where a neighbor man was visiting. When he saw me crying, he started teasing me and snickering. Mama tried to quiet him by telling him what had happened to me that day, but that only made him laugh even more.

I stormed up to my room and stayed until he left. Then I came down to the kitchen. By this time, Hemming had returned from work, and Mama had told him what the man had done.

Mama put her arm around my shoulders and spoke softly.

"It's all right to cry, dear. You just realized you had passed a milestone in your life. Now you will be called a young woman, but still, sometimes you will feel like and want to be a little girl. This growing-up business is very confusing, but then again, so is life." When she finished talking, something else happened that confused me even more. Hemming got up from his chair, came over, put his arm around my shoulders, and spoke. "Welcome to the adult world!"

The expression on my face must have been priceless because when I looked at Mama, she had tears in her eyes.

"Thank you," I stuttered.

Hemming smiled and went back to his chair to light a cigarette. Mama invited me to sit down at the table and have a cup of coffee with them. Mama and Hemming started talking about the prospect of my getting confirmed in the church. They hoped the church would accept me despite my young age. The church did mention that I might not fully understand what I was getting into, but it accepted me anyway. I would start Bible school the following spring.

One evening as I prepared for bed, I heard a knock on my door. "Come in," I called out.

Mama entered, asking if she could speak with me.

I sat on the bed and waited for the lecture. She looked ready to give about something or other I might have done that had rubbed Hemming the wrong way. Mama looked at me with those intense blue eyes of hers.

"I have been watching you studying Hemming when he isn't looking," she began, "and I wonder what you think about him. I have noticed you are very cold toward him. He wants to be your friend, but you will not reach out to him. Randi, dear, he has come to learn to love you a lot, but he's been a bachelor for a long time. Now he has to learn how to have young people in the house, and he has to take it slowly, so he is starting with learning to love you."

I thought about this for an instant.

"But I feel he is trying to take Papa's place by your side, Mama," I replied. "Nobody will be able to take your Papa's place in my heart!" Mama cried. "He was my first love because he gave me your brother, Arvid, then you. When you grow older you will know what I am talking about now. As a woman, I have special needs for companionship from men, and this is why I enjoy Hemming's friendship so much."

A cold hand of fear gripped my insides. I decided to ask Mama a couple of blunt questions.

"Do you love him? Do you sleep with him?"

Mama looked down at her hands and blushed like I had never seen her do before, then looked straight at me when she answered "Yes" to both questions.

I just sat there with an empty feeling.

"Will you stop loving me because I have decided to make a little happiness for us?" Mama asked.

"No," I answered quietly, almost to myself.

Mama got up, kissed me on the cheek goodnight, and went back downstairs. I lay there thinking for the longest time, but I could not get my thoughts in order; they were whirling around and around and dancing in my head. Finally, I drifted off to sleep.

When I saw Hemming the next day, I just couldn't look into his eyes. I still felt he had some devious desire to take Papa's place, and just knowing he and Mama was sharing the same bed made me deeply ashamed.

The next spring I entered Bible school along with the rest of my class. The course, which was to last eleven weeks, would be taught by the bishop of our state, a mild-spoken, gentle old man with bushy eyebrows and a thin ring of grey hair just above his ears.

The bishop was of average height with just the beginnings of a potbelly, but we knew he was an avid skier and walker. During the eleven weeks of Bible class, I grew to love this gentleman of God very much, particularly his sense of humor. As for myself, I have a very macabre sense of humor.

One day in class, I was watching a fly buzzing around the room. As the bishop paced back and forth in front of the students, I began to wonder what would happen if the fly landed on his head. He kept pacing and talking, then would stop to look at us through his horn-rimmed glasses.

When the fly landed right on his glasses, I couldn't help snickering to myself. As the bishop continued walking back and forth, the fly followed him and landed on his head several times. My snickering grew louder in spite of myself, and now a few other students had joined in.

Abruptly, the bishop stopped speaking in mid-sentence. "What is all the snickering about?" he demanded in a rough voice.

The bishop set his sharp eyes on me and commanded me to stand up. I stood up with shaky knees, a little worried about what he was going to say or do.

"Get up on your desk, fly off, and land here," he ordered, pointing to his head, "and if you can't do that, be quiet, please!"

The class broke up in laughter. When the laughter died down, the bishop had another idea.

"I did get a little stuffy, didn't I?" he asked. "Let's take our books and go for a walk, all of us!"

We climbed to the top of a small hill that had a view of the ocean inlet and finished our lesson there, this time with our full attention.

The weeks passed by quickly, and before I knew it, it was Confirmation Sunday. I was a bundle of nerves. The night before, I washed and set my hair in pin curls, but I didn't sleep much, partly from excitement and partly because the bobby pins were poking at my scalp. I got up early and had breakfast with Mama and Hemming.

They conversed about daily things, and I acted like an obedient child and kept quiet, even though I was upset that they weren't mentioning the big event of the day.

Then it was time to get dressed. I was to wear my first long dress, a present from an aunt of Papa, who lived in America. The dress was the most beautiful creation I had ever seen, made of pink silk with white dotted Swiss organza over it. Narrow pink satin ribbon edged in Amsterdam lace highlighted the neck, sleeves, and pockets.

Mama did my hair, and I felt pretty—no, I was pretty! I knew once again that nobody had a dress quite like mine. How could they? It wasn't even made in Norway.

When I walked to church that morning in my new long dress and coat and patent leather shoes, I felt the whole village was looking out their windows at me with envy. I smiled and waved at anybody who looked at me, while I felt as if I was walking ten feet off the ground.

Before we took our vows, there was a very lengthy sermon, then it was our turn. The church was packed—people were standing along the walls—and I felt proud standing in front of the altar, facing the congregation. I didn't really have stage fright, though. Off and on since I was about nine, Mama would write songs for weddings and other festivities, which we would sing in harmony together, accompanied by her on her guitar. But this was a little different; one might say I was "soloing" this one.

The bishop stood up and started asking us questions from the Bible that we were supposed to snap the answer to. I started shaking, and my knees started knocking together. Grabbing the hand of the girl standing next to me, I held on tight and knew she was as scared as I was; both hands were icy cold. When she glanced at me and squeezed back, I knew things would be okay from then on.

As the bishop came toward me, I thought wildly, "Oh, no, not yet, I am not ready!" but oh, yes, he asked me to tell him and the rest of the congregation what the Holy Trinity was as written in the Bible. I opened my mouth, but nothing came out. I tried to clear my throat, but there was nothing to clear. Finally, the correct words came out. When I was done, I looked at the bishop and saw a smile twinkle in those clear blue eyes that rested under those bushy eyebrows. I knew he had seen panic in my eyes. The girl holding my hand squeezed it, and the boy on my other side brushed my hand with his hand. When it was all over, we left the church through the side door to go out in front and wait for the congregation to congratulate us.

There we stood shivering in the cool spring air, receiving handshake after handshake. After we said our goodbyes, we walked to our homes where we were to host our first adult party and could stay up as late as we wanted. I had invited some family friends and relatives, along with one of my best friends who was a year younger than I and would graduate the following year.

Mama baked a traditional cake that tasted heavenly, with fruit filling and loads of whipped cream on top. We also had coffee, hot chocolate, and open-faced sandwiches.

At 10 P.M., after everyone had left, I changed my clothes and decided to go for a walk. When I came down the road a bit from our house, I discovered that the rest of the confirmation class had the same idea- to get some fresh air. We all walked together for about an hour, talking about the day's events, until one girl said she was exhausted and was going home. The rest of us admitted to the same, said goodnight, and headed home.

A few months passed, and then Mama asked me to sit down one day.

"I need to talk to you," she said.

In the pit of my stomach, I felt as if there was a knot-tying contest. Mama fixed us each a cup of coffee, then sat down across the kitchen table from me. She lit a cigarette and inhaled deeply. Finally, she started talking to me.

"I've been really lonely since your Papa died, Randi," she began. "Until we moved here to Bugoynes, I felt that I needed a man."

I thought to myself that this all sounded familiar, that I had heard all this before when we had our "girl talk" up in my bedroom some months back. I let her continue without interruption. There must be a point to this, I thought.

"Have you stopped loving Papa?" I asked bluntly.

"No, Randi, your Papa was my first love and will always be special in my heart." Mama paused, then went on.

"Would you mind having a little brother or sister?" she asked uncertain.

I was so shocked I tipped over my coffee cup, but I didn't even notice! I just stared at Mama in disbelief.

"Do I have a choice?" I asked finally. Mama shook her head. With my insides as cold as ice, I leaned over the table and said, "How could you spit on Papa's grave like this!" and then fled from the kitchen.

Grabbing my coat in the hall, I went out and headed straight for the hills where I knew I wouldn't have to meet anyone. I sat down on a rock and cried. How could she let that man touch her? I thought. I sat there for what seemed like hours, trying to understand.

But I also had a certain unexplainable feeling, possibly respect, for Hemming and his quiet ways. Every morning, he would get up at about 5:30 and work hard all day at the shipyard until he returned home smelling of fresh-cut wood and the special sealer they used to fix leaky fishing boats with. I loved those smells. All this raced through my mind until I finally concluded that maybe it wouldn't be so bad to have a little brother or sister to spoil rotten, but a cold chill still gripped my heart—what if Mama didn't make it through the birth? With her handicap, there was a chance that both she and the baby could die. I threw aside that thought with a "wait-and-see" promise to myself.

When I got home, I noticed that Hemming had returned from work and it was time for supper. As we took our places at the table, I asked if I could speak.

"Yes, Randi," Hemming said and put down his knife and fork. I felt very important at that instant, as a judge handing down a verdict might feel.

"When is the baby due, Mama?" I asked.

"Around April 19th," she answered, never taking her eyes off me. I turned to Hemming.

"Do you love Mama, or was it an accident?" I asked. Hemming's face turned bright red, he shuffled his feet and cleared his throat before he announced his intentions.

"I have come to love and care for your mother very much," he said. "We decided it would be nice to have a child together."

I loved the suspense I had created but decided to let them off the hook.

"I would love to have a baby in the house," I said with a smile.

Mama smiled through tears and Hemming was so embarrassed that he didn't know what to do.

As time went by, Mama had a few minor problems. She was a few pounds overweight, so her blood pressure rose a bit, and she retained a lot of water. Since she had been born with both hip sockets out of joint, her pelvis was slightly crooked, which worried her doctor; he was afraid that she might not be able to give birth to a full-term baby again.

But Mama followed the doctor's orders throughout her pregnancy and did all right. Hemming walked on air.

Chapter 4

As the months went by, my friendships with six people from my confirmation class grew stronger and stronger. Before graduation, they hadn't really wanted me around because of the language barrier. It was a bother to them to speak Norwegian; they figured that it was enough to have to speak it in the classroom, as Mr. Hov didn't allow any Finnish there, which pleased me immensely.

Since Hemming had started helping me learn a few daily words and phrases so that I could begin to understand parts of sentences, I hadn't let on to the group that I understood enough now to know what they were talking about. One evening I met up with the group, and while we were making small talk, one of the girls remarked to me. I understood part of what she was saying and asked her to repeat what she said to me in Norwegian this time. She said something else, and I corrected her. At that, she blushed and left the group. Days later she came to me and apologized in her way, and we became good friends. From then on, no one spoke much Finnish around me. They just weren't sure how much I had learned.

One of the boys singled me out. Kare would make sure I got home alright and would always direct his conversation toward me. One evening he asked me to go steady with him. I answered "Yes" because it was so exciting. Imagine that—my first boyfriend here!

Kare had dark blond hair and a nice open smile. He stood one head taller than I and was very soft-spoken. Much to his mother's dismay, we dated for about 6 or 7 months. She was the official village gossip and also ruled the roost—it didn't matter what her husband said; she said and did as she pleased. Kare was illegitimate—her husband had married her to give him a name.

Kare's father was tall, lanky, and very shy, while his mother was a short, mousy person whom nobody cared for. Because of her sharp tongue, everyone tried to stay on her good side.

Kare's mother didn't like me for two reasons—I lived at Hemming's house and I hadn't been born in Bugoynes. I had also taken an instant dislike to her. She would start all kinds of gossip about me, just to try to break Kare and me up, but nothing held water.

At Christmas, Kare gave me a beautiful necklace made of gold with a real pearl hanging in a net of gold threads. It was lovely!

By the middle of March, the doctor decided to put Mama in the hospital. She had been having problems, and he was a little worried about her and the baby. This meant I would have to take charge of the house and be a hostess for the people who came to do business with Hemming. I was confident that I could do it because I had watched Mama doing the same thing a multitude of times. Months back, Hemming had been contracted by the state to build a harbor pilot boat. When it was nearing completion, a party would have to be given in honor of the event. It was scheduled for April 19, 1952, at our house. I was very busy cleaning, baking a cake, and making open-face sandwiches.

Mr. Asgard, the harbor pilot, was the guest of honor, and the crew who had worked on the boat were also present. We were all sitting in the living room, drinking coffee and sipping glasses of coffee liqueur (for being such a good hostess—Hemming gave me one too) when the telephone rang. It was Mama's doctor at the hospital.

At the solemn sound of his voice, my heart went cold. He asked to speak with Hemming.

Hemming listened for a while, then said, "Thank you," and hung up the receiver.

"I'm a father—I've got a son," he said quietly, staring at each of us.

Then the party really got going! We all let out a yell and started clapping.

When everyone had left, I started clearing the table.

"Leave it until the morning, Randi, and come and sit down with me," Hemming said. He lit a cigarette and sat and smoked for a while.

"Now that I have a son, I would like to have a daughter, too, if she'll accept me," Hemming took my hand, and I saw tears in his eyes.

"You don't have to call me Papa until you are ready, just let me know if you can accept me as your guardian. I'm not trying to take your father's place because I know I cannot. Think about this and give me your answer when you are ready." Hemming squeezed my hand, said goodnight, and went to bed.

After he left the room, I was in shock. I thought I needed something to end the evening with, so I had my first cigarette and my second glass of liquor, which made me promptly throw up. I decided those two vices were not for me and went to bed.

Mama stayed in the hospital for four weeks. The doctor had to make sure that both the baby and Mama would be all right. The birth had been long and laborious and had left Mama weak. Since the hospital was six hours away by boat, the doctor didn't want to take any chances. Finally, Mama called to tell us the doctor had given his permission for her to return home. The following day Hemming took the ferry to pick her up.

I stayed home and cleaned everything spick-and-span. This was their time to be alone, just Mama, Hemming, and the baby, I thought with a smile.

When they arrived home that evening and I saw the baby for the first time, I thought he was the most beautiful creature I had ever seen. I promised myself I would take care of him and help Mama as much as I possibly could.

Mama and Hemming named him Sten. In the months following his birth, I spoiled him terribly. Sten loved every minute of it, but Mama wasn't as thrilled.

As a present for the seven weeks I had spent taking care of the house, Mama gave me 150 kroner or $50.00, a large sum of money in those days. She also bought me a beautiful suit which cost another 150 kroner. It was made of soft grey wool with multicolored pastel bands around the skirt and the bottom of the jacket, and I was very proud of it. Hemming also thought I looked very pretty in it.

I remembered the little talk we had while Mama was in the hospital and thought I had better give him my answer, so I walked down to the shipyard one day with that in mind. I wanted to speak to Hemming alone without Mama happening upon us.

I found Hemming up and said, "I have something I would like to say to you."

He led me into his office and sat down, busying himself with wiping off his hands.

"Remember the little talk we had, you and I?" I began.

He nodded and looked at me with questioning eyes.

"I have decided to give my acceptance to you as my guardian."

Hemming gave me a big smile and said, "Thank you," then got up from his chair, a signal that our meeting was over. While walking home, I wondered what he was feeling right now. When I walked in the door, Mama wanted to know what I had to do at the shipyard. I just smiled and said that I just wanted to see what was going on down there.

After this trip to the yard, I found myself going down there more often. The men who worked there would always ask me if I wanted anything, but my answer would always be "No." I became very interested in how the work was done, how boats were built, plank by plank, and what kept them from leaking once they were in the water. All these questions needed answers, and Hemming would take time out of his busy day to answer them. At one time, Mama became suspicious of my spending so much time at the shipyard. I told her of my interests, but she thought my interests really centered around a young apprentice who worked there. One night at the dinner table, she gently brought up the subject. When Hemming told her of all my questions, along with the fact that I hadn't even looked toward the young man at all, she seemed satisfied with the explanation.

When Sten was one year old, Mama decided I should travel to southwestern Norway to visit her brother, Uncle Magnar, with the possibility of staying down there and working. The idea fascinated me. It meant I would have to leave my boyfriend, but that didn't bother me too much; our relationship had cooled quite a bit during the last four weeks. He was a bit of a stick in the mud and I was the strict opposite. He didn't dance, I taught him—in short, I didn't like the odds. When I told him I wanted out of our relationship, he seemed shocked, but I decided to be nice about it and let it go.

The days went by quickly as I readied myself for my journey—packing clothes and doing other chores that needed to be done before I left. To get to my destination, I would have to travel five days by steamship, but that wasn't going to be a problem since Mama's Uncle Albert worked as a purser on the steamship she had chosen, The Finnmarken.

Uncle Albert promised me free meals on the trip in exchange for some light-duty work. Mama saw me off on the ferry that would take me to Kirkenes where I was to catch the steamship. As she said goodbye, she kissed me on my cheek and begged me to be careful. Mama had tears in her eyes, but I kissed her back, hugged her, and told her not to worry. On the ferry, I kept thinking about the look in her eyes and her parting words, never realizing how true this would sound later.

When I walked up the gangway of The Finnmarken, Uncle Albert was there to meet me and take me to my cabin.

"What should I call you?" I asked.

"How about calling me Uncle Albert like your Mama does!" He was a quiet man in his late 50s, tall and lean. His hair had flecks of grey, and thick eyebrows showed over his horn-rimmed glasses. Although Uncle Albert had a soft voice, it had a certain command in it.

"You will be rooming with another girl," he said as we reached my cabin. "Take tonight to relax. You'll start working tomorrow morning at eight sharp. See you at dinner; it will be served as soon as we leave port."

I smiled and thanked him as he left. A little while later, my roommate came in. She was a pretty girl with shoulder-length jet-black hair, brown eyes rimmed with long, curled lashes, a fair complexion, and an hourglass figure with an extra-large bosom. I smiled to myself, thinking that I wouldn't stand out on the ship with my own larger than normal bosom.

"I'm Kari," she said, "and I've been asked to help you out on the first day of your duties."

As we talked for a while, I discovered that Kari was a very likable 20-year-old girl. She explained that my duties would be to check cabins for forgotten articles after guest departures, change the linen, and ensure that the cabins were clean.

I had fun getting acquainted with the crew during the first couple of days on board. I even discovered a schoolmate from my birthplace who was working on the ship. Roald was surprised to see me, and I got caught up on all that had happened in the village since I had left. I also met a cook named Atle, who was about 22, with dark blond hair and blue eyes. He seemed to take a liking to me, which worried me a little because I often caught him staring at me, but I wasn't afraid. On the fourth evening on board, I was in my cabin when there was a knock on the door. I was alone and thought it was Kari, so I opened the door. There stood Atle with a smile on his face, asking if he could come in and talk, explaining that he had a message from my uncle. I said, "Okay," but I wasn't prepared for what happened next. When Atle came in, he closed the door behind him and locked it! Right away, he began feeling me all over and telling me what a beautiful body I had with my large, full bosom. I was getting scared and wanted to scream, but he laid his hand over my mouth, threw me on the bed, and raped me! When he was done, he got up, pointed his finger at me, and told me not to say a word to anyone.

"I'll start rumors about you on the ship and shatter that sweet girl image you're portraying," he hissed. "Your Uncle Albert will probably tell your mother about it." Atle went on and on. Since I was so unknowing about these sorts of things, I believed him. I just knew that when I went to work the next morning, everyone would see it in me, the guilt and everything. As soon as I heard him close the door, I jumped up and locked it, then feverishly stripped off my clothes and started washing, trying to wash his lingering touch off along with all my guilt. All the while tears were streaming down my face. Thoughts were racing through my mind, one in particular — that my life as I had known it, with my happy-go-lucky attitude, was over. I felt like I was all alone in the world with my shame.

I put on my nightgown, turned out the light, and went to bed, but I couldn't sleep. I just stared out into the darkness. I don't know how long I had been doing this when Kari came back. She sounded happy and was humming to herself. I felt her eyes on me, but I pretended to be sleeping. I felt so ashamed that I couldn't tell her or anyone else what had happened to me that evening.

After a sleepless night, I got up very early the following morning, about 5:30. I was thankful that the ship would be docking at 9:00 and I could finally escape Atle. But those thoughts didn't really help the way I felt. I gave myself a sponge bath once again because I still felt incredibly dirty, but it didn't help. I did my job automatically, then went to my cabin to pack. When I said goodbye to Kari, we hugged each other and made promises to keep in touch. I found Uncle Albert in his office.

"Thank you for everything," I told him. He smiled. "I've had good reports on your work, Randi," he said. "As long as I'm the purser on board, there's always a job for you here." As I left his office, I thought with sadness, why couldn't things have been different? I could have worked on the ship all summer and had a lot of fun on top of it.

At 9:00 AM, we docked in Bergen. Since Kari had gone back to sleep (she didn't have to leave the ship until noon), I gathered my things as quietly as possible. I watched Kari sleep, thinking about what a good friend she had become in the short time I had known her. I had an impulse to wake her, tell her how terrific I thought she was, and warn her about Atle and the kind of guy he was.

I was still so upset that I didn't even go to find Roald to tell him goodbye and to ask him to send greetings to all my old friends. If I did see Roald, I was afraid I would break down and tell him what had happened. Roald would probably beat Atle up; he was honorable and didn't believe in any nonsense. But I just wiped a tear from my eye and slipped quietly off the ship.

Once ashore, I hailed a taxi to the ferry that would take me to Stavanger and Uncle Magnar. I boarded the ferry early—one hour before departure—and sat down next to a window to do some thinking. Uncle Albert had been so nice to me. He wanted me to stay, but I wonder what he would have said if he had known what had taken place. He probably would have kicked me off the ship. In those days in Norway, it was a shame for a girl to have a mark like that, yet all the boy got was a slap on the wrist, at least that was what I had heard. Girls that came from Finnmark, the northern part of Norway, had it especially rough. People in the south called them trash, and during World War II even circulated rumors that the people of Finnmark were covered with hair and had tails hidden in their clothing. They said it had something to do with the frigid air.

These rumors stuck with us up into the early 1950s, which was why I couldn't say a word to anyone; coming from Finnmark, nobody would have believed me or would have just smiled and walked away.

The ferry pulled away from the dock for our two-and-a-half-hour trip. It snaked in and out of the picturesque fjords of the state of Hordaland, where the scenery changes from mountains to rolling hills dotted with houses in bright colors among green trees. I didn't see any of this; I just sat there.

As I stared out into space and smoked one cigarette after another, Mama's parting words echoed through my mind. Did she have a premonition about what was to happen to me, or was it "mother's intuition"?

When we finally docked at Stavanger, Uncle Magnar met me at the dock. I hadn't seen him since Papa's funeral, but he looked the same, as handsome as ever with the same blue eyes as Mama and dark wavy hair. When he smiled, his eyes would close, and his whole face would light up.

Stavanger is a very beautiful coastal city that sprawls over a hillside and the coastal inlet. Uncle Magnar and I made small talk as he drove us to his house about a half-hour away, and I began to feel at ease. He told me that Frank and Viggo, his two sons, were waiting impatiently for my arrival. When he mentioned that Aunt Maiken would probably have dinner ready, I realized that I hadn't eaten since breakfast, but I wasn't really very hungry.

We pulled up in front of a small, two-story white house. Walking into the front hall, I saw just how small it was — to the left was a kitchen, to the right a bedroom, and ahead was a steep stair that led to the second floor. I entered the kitchen, where I met Aunt Maiken. She was just as beautiful as I remembered her, with classic features and a perfectly chiseled profile, bright blue eyes framed with long black eyelashes, and a lovely little mouth. When she smiled, her face lit up just like Uncle Magnar's. Both of their voices were very soft, and they never raised them, no matter what happened.

After I had lived there for a few weeks, I started looking for a job. I found one as a housekeeper for a very wealthy couple whose children were grown. They lived in a three-story house with a retail store on the first floor and living quarters on the second. They had closed off the third floor when their children had left, and now used it only for the holidays.

Mr. Hansen was a soft-spoken man with gentle features and a big stomach. He always wore a grey suit with a vest that had a watch in one pocket with a gold chain attached to another pocket. He constantly puffed on a big cigar. Mrs. Hansen was a bit overweight also but was a nice and gentle woman who always had a smile ready. She had very wavy hair that she wore in a large bun. When she went shopping, she would put on her mink coat and hat and fur-lined boots and stay out all day. She always brought me back something special — a piece of candy or cake from the tea salon, always some little thing — so needless to say, I felt very happy working there.

As the weeks went by, I felt my old self starting to come back. I had put some of the bad thoughts to rest, but I still had an uneasy feeling about something; I wasn't sure what.

When that time of month came, nothing happened. I thought I'd wait a couple of days; maybe the rape, plus the new surroundings, had delayed my monthly cycle. After a week had passed and nothing had happened, I had to face the truth. I was sure I was pregnant and decided I had to talk to somebody about this deep shame I was carrying.

I knew I couldn't tell anybody else except my family, so I went to my aunt and uncle and told them the whole story. When I had finished, I felt such relief to get this off my chest that I started crying. Aunt Maiken and Uncle Magnar led me to the couch, put their arms around me, and let me cry it out.

"It must have been awful for you to not be able to tell anybody and still be able to be so light and cheery," Aunt Maiken said. "You never let anyone see how you were suffering inside."

"I'll take you to our doctor and have you checked out," Uncle Magnar assured me.

Sure enough, I was pregnant. According to the size of the fetus, I had conceived around the time of the rape. After the examination, the doctor asked me if I wanted to keep the baby.

"No," I said without hesitation.

"Well, it's your decision," he said.

He gave me some pills to take at regular intervals. But nothing happened when I took them, not even any spotting of blood. I just got very sick for several days.

Uncle Magnar called the doctor, but he said there was nothing more that he could do.

"We should call your Mama and tell her about this," Uncle Magnar said. "Maybe you should go home."

But since I had arrived at my uncle's house, I had found a boyfriend and was so in love that the thought of leaving him behind was shattered. Harry played the accordion in Uncle Magnar's quartet that performed at dances every Saturday night. He demanded to know why I was leaving. I had to tell him, but I felt so ashamed I couldn't look him in the eyes. He put his arms around me and said it was all right. Deep down, I was hoping he would ask me to marry him. I would daydream about caring for him and the baby in our own little home, but I knew it wouldn't happen. It was hard to say goodbye to Harry, but I had to.

The only thing left to do was to tell my employer that I was leaving. Mr. and Mrs. Hansen had been so kind that I hated to tell them. Sometimes when I had been working, I would feel awful and not be able to keep any food down. Mrs. Hansen would make me a special tea that always calmed my stomach and urged me to relax until I felt strong enough to continue my work.

Sometimes she would even pitch in and work with me. On the morning of my last day, I sat on the bus to her house and rehearsed my speech to her. When I arrived, I asked to speak with her right away. We went into her beautiful kitchen where she poured us a cup of coffee and set out some pastries. As I told her my story, that my mother needed me at home and I had to leave, Mrs. Hansen kept watching my face. She didn't say anything, and I was wondering what she was thinking. We got up from the table, and she came over to me and gave me a big hug. She smelled like sweet soap. It smelled so good that I wanted it to stay like that forever. Then she looked searchingly into my eyes.

"When is your baby due?" she asked.

I felt my face go red. "April, I guess," I stammered.

"I know that there is a lot more to this than you will tell me," Mrs. Hansen said, "but I won't ask. If you want to tell me, you can."

But I couldn't; a lump in my throat prevented me from getting the words out. I wished I could stay there with her, but I knew that was impossible.

"You don't have to work today, Randi," Mrs. Hansen said. "Let's sit down and have an all-day 'girl talk.'"

So, we sat and talked for hours. She showed me pictures of her children and grandchildren, and before I knew it, the clock on the mantle struck twelve, and it was time for lunch.

Mr. Hansen came to have lunch with us, then retired for a nap. As Mrs. Hansen worked on her embroidery and I sat beside her, I thought that maybe I should tell her what had happened to me so she wouldn't think I was one of those "loose" girls. She listened quietly to my sad story. When I finally ran out of words and was sitting there looking at my hands in my lap, Mrs. Hansen reached over and took my hands in hers and looked at me with tears in her eyes.

"My God, child, how you must have suffered in these past weeks!" she cried.

I suddenly sank to my knees and put my head in her lap and cried until I had no more tears, while Mrs. Hansen sat there stroking my hair. When I stopped crying, I apologized for my outburst.

"No, you needed someone to talk to who was not family," Mrs. Hansen said kindly, "you needed to speak and be yourself. There's no need for apologies." She thought for a moment.

"What will you do now?" she asked.

"I guess I'll go home and have my baby there," I answered.

"What will be done to the boy who did this to you? He shouldn't get away with it, you know!"

"I guess I will talk about it with Mama and Papa," I said.

"Smart move on your part," Mrs. Hansen smiled.

I looked at the clock on the mantle and realized it was time for me to leave. Mrs. Hansen told me to wait; she said she had to pay me for my work.

"But I didn't work today!" I protested.

Mrs. Hansen lifted a finger and said, "Tsk, tsk, you need the money now more than ever, so here you are," stuck some bills in my hand and closed my hand around them.

"There's no need for thanks; buy something for the baby," she said.

I gave her a hug and a kiss on the cheek and said goodbye. By this time Mr. Hansen had arisen from his nap. Mrs. Hansen told him I was going home. He came over to me and shook my hand and told me goodbye.

"It's been so nice to have you here, Randi," he said. "You've been like a breath of young, fresh air. Having you around made me miss my own children less."

He took out his wallet, pulled some money out, and stuck it in my other hand, then turned and went back to the living room. I stood there with my mouth open in surprise.

"Mustn't miss your bus, dear," Mrs. Hansen said with a smile. "Have a good trip home, and God bless you, child."

After one more hug, I left and she closed the door behind me.

On the bus home, I counted the money they had given me, and to my surprise, it was 500 kroner, about $500! I thought of our conversation when I had said I needed to talk to Mama and 'Papa'. This meant that I had accepted Hemming as my father within my heart, but what would he think of his new daughter now?

When I got to Uncle Magnar's house, I found out that Mama had wired me money for my ticket home. Two days later I was on my way. I caught a different steamship this time because I didn't dare to face Uncle Albert again.

The trip was anything but fun. I was seasick all the way home so I stayed in my cabin. "This is odd," I thought, "I've never been seasick before, but now my whole system seems upside down."

When the ferry docked at Bugoynes, both Mama and Hemming were there to take me home, which was odd, I thought. We greeted each other politely and I knew we had a long and probably emotional talk ahead of us. When we got home, they let me relax for a while. Hemming brought my luggage up to my room and I unpacked. We had returned at 5:00 P.M., and — as always — the evening meal was on the table promptly at 8:00. We ate in silence, and when we had finished, I turned to Hemming and apologized for bringing this into his house. When I told him what actually had happened, he got visibly upset and asked me to get up from my chair. My heart grew cold.

I got up, and he pulled the chair over next to him and asked me to sit down again. Then Hemming put his arm around my shoulders and said, "What did you think I would do when you confronted me — throw you out? That has never entered my mind."

"I've been a bachelor all my life, Randi, and now that I'm 48 years old, I have a full-fledged family to take care of. I promise to defend and care for you just as if you were my own flesh and blood."

That did it. I started crying, and oh, it felt so good to cry it all out as Hemming sat there with his arm around my shoulders.

Throughout this, Mama had kept quiet, but now she cleared her throat to speak.

"Now we are a family," she said softly.

I looked at her and saw tears rolling down her cheeks. Needless to say, Hemming's behavior surprised me, because I had made up my mind from the first day I saw him too intensely, and I disliked him. As far as I was concerned, he had no qualities for me to call him a friend or, heaven forbid, "Father." Now I was very confused about what to do. He had been honest with me, so maybe he wasn't all that bad. Right then, I was too tired and worn out to worry or to try to reason with anything. I would have plenty of time for that in the long winter months to come.

Suddenly, I felt a soft touch on my arm and looked down to see my little brother Sten wanting "Sissa," his name for me. I picked him up and hugged him gladly; I had missed him so much. Sten and I sat and made small talk for a while. Before he went to bed, I told him I couldn't wait until the next day when the two of us would go for a walk. Imagine! He would become an uncle at two years old.

It wasn't long before I started to show my condition. To keep the tongues from wagging in the village, I wore Mama's old wedding band that Papa had given her; we had it shined up at the jeweler's so it looked new. People wanted to know where my fiancé was and where we had met, so I told them that we had met in Stavanger and that he was sailing in the merchant marines. All through those nine months, I stuck to that story.

My old boyfriend Kare made some sly remark that I had gotten "knocked up" because I was easy. That hurt me terribly because I thought he was my friend, he and the old gang. The first chance I got, I gave him back the necklace made of gold with the pearl that he had given me. I told him I didn't appreciate what I had heard, and that I had guessed wrong when I thought he was my friend. On that note, I turned on my heel and left him standing there.

After I had walked a few yards, I looked over my shoulder at him. To my amusement, he was still standing in the same spot, looking at the necklace with a mixture of surprise, sadness, and disbelief on his face.

I saw Kare on a Saturday morning. That night, he got roaring drunk and sat on the dock with his best friend Emil. Suddenly Kare started crying, pulled out the necklace, tore it into little pieces, and then threw it into the sea.

"I didn't do it, I didn't do it," he cried. "I could never do anything that cruel to her. I still love her and would do anything to keep anybody from hurting her in the condition she is in. She must really be hurting inside from all the vicious gossip."

Emil suggested that they try to stop all the gossip about me that was going around. As time went on, they did their best to try.

A few days after Kare's outburst, I met Emil while I was taking my daily walk. He told me what had happened at the dock that night. I felt bad about what I had done.

"Don't worry about it, Randi," Emil assured me. "Kare will come around. We're going to try to find out who is starting all this gossip."

One by one, all my girlfriends stopped visiting me. Not only did I not want to be seen out with the gang, but we just had nothing in common anymore. They didn't want to be seen going to our house or associating with me because of all the gossip.

There was one exception. A girl I had least expected to stand by me or be my friend made an effort to support and defend me whenever she heard gossip. Anne was the same age as I was but was one year behind me in school (I had graduated a year ahead for my age). She was never really a part of our gang, but I thought the world of her. Tall and slim, with dark curly hair and blue eyes, Anne stood by me all the way through.

As the months went by and I grew larger and larger, the gossip finally died down. One day I was out on my daily walk when I met Kare on the road. He greeted me and asked if we could meet later, after dark. I agreed.

Chapter 5

When I got home, I discussed this meeting with Mama. She urged me to meet with Kare, so that evening I did. He stood there shuffling his feet, and I detected nervousness, so I suggested that we go for a walk to the dock where we could sit down before going home again. For the last few days, it had been snowing heavily over a layer of black ice, so Kare grabbed a hold of my arm so I wouldn't slip and fall. When we got to the dock, we found a place to sit down. Kare offered me a cigarette.

"No, thank you," I said. "It makes my stomach uneasy. I guess it's because I'm pregnant."

"Do you mind if I smoke?" Kare asked.

"No, go right ahead. It doesn't bother me if someone else is smoking. As you know, both Mama and Hemming smoke."

Kare sat there smoking quietly. Finally, he cleared his throat.

"Please believe me when I say to you that I never started any gossip," he said sincerely. "I could never do that because I still like you a lot. Please tell me one thing, is your fiancé coming to get you and your baby once you have given birth?"

I knew then that I could trust Kare, so I told him the whole terrible story. When I had finished, he sat there for a moment. Then he jumped up and started hitting his fist against the wall.

"Dammit! How can any guy do anything like this to a decent girl like you, or anybody else for that matter? It just isn't fair!"

Kare sat down again and grabbed my hand, which was icy from nervousness. I had never seen him like that before.

"When you have your baby, what will you do?" he asked.

"I don't know yet," I answered uncertain.

Kare kissed me on the cheek and said, "You have always been nice and cheery to everybody. Don't ever lose that. But right now, I think you are cold. Let me walk you home."

We stopped again when we got to the gate in front of my house.

"Oh, by the way, I found out who the main gossiper is. Rest assured, that person will not say another word, not about you, anyway!" Kare squeezed my hand and asked hesitatingly if he could see me again. I agreed, and then we said goodnight and parted company.

In my seventh month, I started filling up with fluids. The doctor admitted me to the birthing clinic, where they put me on a salt-free diet which helped a lot with fluid retention. But I was bored stiff staying there. I would go for walks every day, but I was a little afraid of falling since the spring thaw had begun, and there was lots of black ice on the roads. Besides that, it was becoming very uncomfortable for me to walk because I had gotten so big.

One early afternoon, the midwife came to the clinic to examine me. Since I was two weeks overdue, she suggested that she induce labor. I was so tired of lugging that big stomach around (it seemed as if I had been that big for years) that I gladly agreed with her suggestion. She gave me a white powder stirred into warm water to drink, followed by a kind of oil, stirred into warm water. By the time I had drunk all those liquids, I felt absolutely stuffed and started having pains within the hour.

To make the birth easier, the midwife told me to keep walking in the hall until I couldn't walk anymore. I walked for three hours. When I finally couldn't move my feet anymore from all the pain, I was escorted into the birthing room.

It didn't take long! About 20 minutes later, on April 19, 1954, I was the proud mother of a little girl! I named her Evy Christin, a name which had come to me in a dream. In this dream, Grandma Kristine asked me if you were to have a girl, what would I name her? When I said I didn't know, she suggested the name Evy Christin. I thought I had better obey; my baby might have a special blessing bestowed upon her if I did.

Two days after the birth of my Evy, a distant relative of Hemming's came to give birth to twins. She requested a bed in my room. Her name was Hansine.

Hansine's mother-in-law was Hemming's sister-in-law and a very disliked lady. When I was about three months pregnant, she decided she had to find out whether I was pregnant or not. One evening she came to visit my home. She sat down close to the mirror where I was combing my hair and getting ready to go out with my girlfriend Anne. Since it was chilly outside, I had put on a sweater, but I had not buttoned it up all the way. Hemming's sister-in-law ran her hand up under my sweater, laughing and saying "Tickle, tickle," trying to see if my stomach was rigid. I smacked her hand as hard as I could, glared at her, and warned her to stop it. One could have heard a pin drop; it got so quiet then.

After that episode, I wouldn't give this woman the time of day. (My mother thought I was awfully hard on her, seeing that she was family (sort of), but I stood my ground.) Now her daughter-in-law was in my room. I made up my mind: if that woman came to visit, I would go to our special sitting room and wait until she left. Hansine later told me her mother-in-law was puzzled and disappointed that she didn't get to speak with me, but I never offered any explanation. I didn't want Hansine to know what her mother-in-law had done to me; it would have hurt her terribly.

Our babies grew by 'leaps and bounds'. Hansine had twins, a boy, and a girl, and her husband was walking on air. We both breastfed our children, but Hansine did not have enough milk for two and asked if I could help her out. Since I had an abundance of very rich milk, I agreed. Evy only drank a little before she was satisfied, and all the milk I had left made my breasts full and sore.

The midwife suggested that I feed other children whose mothers did not have milk or, like Hansine, didn't have enough. Every eight hours, I would supplement one of Hansine's children, plus another baby boy whose mother didn't get her milk until four days after his birth. Since my milk had come two days after Evy's birth, I was the talk of the birthing clinic with my ample supply that fed three other babies besides my own.

My strength came back quickly. I felt good and wanted to go home, but the midwife suggested that I stay for seven days since I faced a long journey—one and a half hours by boat, then a fifteen-minute walk from the dock. On the morning of the day I was to leave, I visited my other babies. Both mothers had a fair amount of milk by then, so they would be alright. Hemming came to bring me home. When he saw Evy, he smiled and touched her hand. I thought I saw a look of pride in his eyes as he picked her up in his arms and carried her out to the waiting taxi.

I was happy that Evy was such a good baby. One afternoon, two weeks after her birth, I got up from my nap and felt different. My mother took one look at me and immediately knew something was wrong. She called the village practitioner nurse, who came right away and took my temperature, which had risen to 103 degrees. I had no pain, but the nurse went on examining me and found that I had "the fever."

Women used to die of this fever in the 1800s if they got it after childbirth. The nurse called the doctor at the birthing clinic and conferred with him. He sent a special and very expensive medication on the chartered boat to our village which the nurse picked up on the dock. It was a bottle with only eight pills and each pill ran about $10 a pop but we never saw a bill.

I came very close to death, till later but while I was deep in the fever the other thing happened to me. I felt as if someone was making me stand straight up against a wall, while a choir of voices kept yelling;

stand straight, stand straight! I was so tired, all I wanted to do was lie down!

I lost 2 days of my life during the fever; the worst part was what happened to my baby. Before we knew that I had the fever, she drank some of the milk and now she wouldn't wake up. She had to be immersed in lukewarm water to shock her so she could eat. Luckily, we both came through it!

My baby grew fast and was a very happy baby with her blue eyes and curly dark blonde hair. My little brother who was only 2 years older, thought that she should play with him and when he discovered that she slept only he became upset. But when she became a little bit older, he taught her to play with him.

People in the village started gossiping again about me, saying that I would soon start running around.

Papa tipped me off, and I fooled them all, I didn't go out to a dance or anything before my baby was 9 months old. Everyone at the dance was surprised to see me many came over to talk to me. A few young men asked me to dance. Later, a couple of young boys got drunk and started coming on to me, which scared me. Because I didn't want anything to do with men and so, I walked home. When I walked in the door at home, I was shaking like a leaf. Oh, Randi, you look like you saw a ghost! Mama said.

I blurted out the whole story about what happened at the dance. Mama became angry and called them inconsiderate juveniles! But it prevented me from going out for a while.

When my baby was about 4 months old, mama and Papa started prying for information about the baby's father. I really didn't want to talk about it, but would rather forget about the whole mess and just enjoy my little bundle of joy. But Mama made a call to Uncle Albert on board the ferry, she found out about the cook and found that he had quit his job on the ship and signed on with the Merchant Marine. With that information, she went to the police and asked them to track him down. We found out that not only did he have a long rape record but he also had nine other children conceived the same way. I must have been special to him or something, because about a month later I received a letter from him and the letter from his parents who begged me to come and see them so they could see the baby and I could possibly marry their son! Mama handed both letters over to the police and we never heard any more about it.

In Norway, the state pays a monthly stipend for each child a woman has, instead of deducting a tax time like they do in the United States. When Evy was about 10 months old, I started receiving support money, and when she was a year and a half mama and I had another talk.

Randi, you have proven that you don't need any help raising your daughter, she began. How would you like to get yourself a job? Of course she continued, you will have to leave the village but the baby stays here with me and you wouldn't have to worry about her because she'll be well taken care of.

I considered the idea for a couple of weeks, then consented to go with the understanding that if I missed the baby too much, I would return home with no questions asked.

I found a job as a waitress in the Missionary Hotels Cafe in a little town which was a Day's Journey by boat from our village. The hotel manager and his wife were nice, but very straitlaced Christian people who ruled with a firm hand. They hired mostly young people like myself, so they could mold us into perfect employees! Since it was a Christian place, services were held four times a week. Sunday morning and afternoon, Wednesday afternoon, and Saturday evening, and all of the staff were expected to attend but since we were young and not really religious, all we really wanted to do was go dancing and meet young boys. When we did go dancing the cook would spy on us and report to the boss getting us into trouble! Although the cook was only 22 years old, he was deeply religious with almost fanatical thoughts. He thought that since he believed in God, he would change everyone around him, not with gentleness but with Force if necessary! I thought this guy looked like a pig with his straight red hair that stuck out under his Cook's hat, pale complexion, and the big fat nose that resembled the snout and definitely he did not look like a nice person should look!

I met another young girl the same age as me, and one day we decided we had had it with our jobs. Mary was only 17, the same age as me, and a very pretty girl with curly blonde hair and brown eyes and she was full of life and fun! Mary and I quit our jobs and took the steamship down to another town a half-day journey South. When we arrived, I called Mama to tell her what had been going on so she wouldn't worry. Mama told me that the boss at the hotel had called with stories about Mary and me. He called us Jezebels, and said we stayed out all night, and when we came back to the hotel we smelled like alcohol on our breath!

Randi, I told him that you have never taken a drink in your life, but he kept arguing and saying that his cook had told him so! I exploded in laughter and told Mama about the cook, she listened and then assured me that she would set the record straight! Before she hung up, she told me how my baby was doing and I was happy to hear about her because I missed her so much. After I hung up, I wondered what Mama meant by setting the record straight for the manager but I never did find out.

I had a lot of relatives in this new town where we landed Mary and I, so there would be no problem with the place to stay until we found ourselves a job. The day after we arrived, we were hired as live-in housekeepers at an Undertaker's place whose names were Mr. and Mrs. Hulbertson.

The Mrs. was a lovely elderly lady who ruled both her house and her business with a firm hand. But she also had the fun side, and when the cook would make a pot of tea, then we the girls would be invited up to the Parlor where we would sit and eat cake and drink tea while she told a story of her Young Life.

She was a short, plump lady with round glasses that she wore way down on her nose. When she wasn't meeting clients, she would wear a little bonnet with the satin bow tied under her chin. Her voice was light and soft and when she laughed it was so joyful and it sounded like it rolled off her tongue.

Mr. Hulbertson was another matter, he was a balding, corpulent, cigar-puffing man with huge horn rim glasses and a booming voice. As soon as I saw him, I heard a voice warning within me telling me not to be alone with this man, ever! When I asked the cook Margo about him, all she said was-just watch yourself! One day something happened that confirmed my suspicions…

I was in the sewing room doing some mending for myself when suddenly I smelled the odor of cigars. I turned numb as Mr. Hulbertson came from behind and stuck his hand into my blouse to feel my breasts. I immediately backhanded him, but he just smiled and walked off. I sank down on my chair, buried my face in my hands, and cried. Will this ever end? I thought.

I don't know how long I sat there, but eventually, I heard the cooks call for lunch, dried my tears, and went upstairs. When I walked into the kitchen, Margo took one look at me and said, He tried, didn't he?

I just nodded… Margo swore under her breath, that under-sex bastard!

Let me tell you one thing girls, Margo started, he hasn't slept with his wife in 30 years, I guess it's no wonder. But let me try to help you, I will have a talk with Mrs. He's afraid of her, she really is the boss here because she inherited the business from her family.

That evening, Mr. Hulbertson was called into the Parlor and the door closed behind him.

That evening Mary, Margo, and I went out to town to check out the action.

From that point on we were never bothered by Mr. Hulbertson again, so I guess his wife put fear in him, that was all right by me, no I didn't have to look over my shoulder all the time with worry.

Mary and I stayed with the Hulbertsons, although it wasn't much of a job, there was no challenge with hard work but the money wasn't bad.

One evening Mary and I decided to go dancing. A marine frigate had docked in town. This town was a naval stop between the North Sea and Southern Norway. At the frigate, some men stood watch while the rest of them went ashore and came to the dance. One of them asked me to dance, a handsome sailor with wavy blonde hair and The Bluest Eyes I had ever seen. He was a good dancer and we hit it off right away. When the dance was over, he wanted to walk me home, but I declined. The next evening, Mary and I went out again with hopes of meeting the Young Marines by chance. We found the Marines had a little cafe, where we sat down with them and drank coffee and talked until the cafe closed at 11:00, they asked to walk us home to where we lived.

The ship is leaving tomorrow morning, one of them said but will be back in 3 weeks, hoping we can see you too then. I don't know, Mary and I answered in unison.

One of them, Einar, was so gentle that I felt completely at ease with him. 3 weeks went by and the frigate returned from Duty and we invited the boys up to our room.

One morning six weeks later or so, I felt a little funny, hoping I was wrong, but I was not that lucky, I was pregnant once again! The next time I saw Einar, I voiced my suspicion and we went to the telephone station downtown to call his parents.

After we told them the story, they asked him to send me down to his hometown in Western Norway.

Then I called Mama and told her shamefully what was about to happen, but she surprised me.

Einar is doing the only decent thing he can do considering the circumstances," Mama said and continued," Be happy you deserve it dear!" Then she changed the subject to my little daughter. I listened to the stories about her daily antics and started crying and realized that it would be a long time before I would see her again and it had been almost a year since I saw her last time.

My trip to Bergen by steamship went uneventfully. Einar's mother Lina met me at the dock and brought me to her home where Einar's father Hakon, his three brothers, and the grandmother lived. The older brother Harold, was married to a woman named Marlene and lived on the second floor with their young son.

My future father-in-law had been in the German prison camp in Norway during World War II and after the treatment there at the camp did not feel right after the ordeal. Quite often he would feel a terrible cramp in his stomach with pains that made him double over and that would last for hours and then he couldn't eat anything. The doctors came up empty for something to help him with.

The grandmother was my favorite, she was quite a lady, small and gnarled with petite little hands. Because she didn't have much hair, she always wore a knitted cap on her head. What fascinated me was her eyes, each pointed in the opposite direction, and was dark brown almost black. She spoke in the old-world dialect of Bergen so when I first arrived, I had a very difficult time understanding her but as time went by it became easier. Since her legs wouldn't carry her much anymore, she mostly stayed in a room. I used to go in and sit with her for hours on end when everyone was at work and she used to tell me stories of her Youth and all the things that went on. Einar came home on leave, and we decided to get married on New Year's Eve 1955. We were married in the Little Chapel on the island where we lived just outside Bergen. This island was quite unusual, with lots of trees and huge boulders. People had settled along the road and built their houses there. The road had been carved all around the island and every so often you come to a little village of 30 to 50 houses. Every 2 hours we had ferry service from Bergen, and from the ferry bus service all the way around the island.

Chapter 6

The wedding reception went fine until 7:30 when the groom's arch-enemy arrived, raving drunk! He was an old-school chum, and whenever they came together and had been drinking, it never failed, they would end up fighting! But when they met sober, they were the best of buddies. It was a very odd friendship! So, his buddy picked a fight with him, but the buddy was thrown out by the groom's brothers. It didn't matter, for me the reception was ruined! Using the excuse that I was exhausted from being 5 months pregnant, I left the party and went to bed.

Einar served his full Military Time stationed mostly in Bergen. When he was discharged, he came home and fixed up a two-room in the basement of his father's apartment and that's where on June 3rd, 1956 I gave birth to our daughter Katie. The Midwife came to our place and delivered her and all went well. I stayed in bed for 4 days while my sister-in-law took care of us. My husband got a job as a welder at a shipyard where they built freighters. He was earning good money and we lived well and were happy. Katie grew and was healthy until she developed a whooping cough when she was one and a half years old. She stayed in Bergen Hospital for 4 days and came through it all right with no complications. Up to then, Einar had not been doing any drinking to speak of, mostly in the company of his family but now he started hitting the taverns Every payday and on other nights of the week as well. His quitting time at work was 5:00 p.m., but I rarely saw him until 10:30 when he came home with the Last Ferry of the evening. I hated it when he came home drunk, he would be loud and boisterous and demand food on the table! Since we all slept in the living room on the rollout couch, he would usually wake Katie with his loud voice and I would have a difficult time getting her back to sleep again. The following day was no better, he would have a hangover and either stay home all day sleeping or go to work then hit another Tavern after quitting time to do repair work on his head! One evening he came home late again. When I asked him in a quiet friendly voice about his day, he got angry and started slapping me around. I let out the scream and his brothers came running and wrestled him to the floor and held him until he calmed down! I grabbed Katie and went up to his parents to sleep.

A couple of weeks later he was late again, 'why should I sit up and wait for him?' I questioned myself. I packed Katie in the stroller and walked over to a friend's house. When my friend and her husband asked me why I seemed so nervous, I told them what had been going on. They both made me promise to let them know if he ever touched me again in violence. About 7:30 in the evening there was a knock on their door, there he stood about as drunk as you can get swaying back and forth and wondering if I was there. I said a hurried goodbye and started home with him but I was really scared of the look in his eyes. I knew that he wouldn't hurt Katie in any way, he loved her much too much for that, but she could accidentally get in the way and he would blame me for her injury. I just made it in the front door when he caught me by the hair and started hitting me. Katie began screaming and I knew I was in for it. He kept hitting and kicking me and finally, I knew that the only way to draw attention to my plight was to scream and scream I did, down came his brothers once again led by the oldest one it took all four of them to pull him off of me. As they held him down, because he had to teach me a lesson in how to care for a husband and have his food ready when he came home from work tired and hungry. I grabbed Katie and went back upstairs to his parents once again, my only refuge. This time he had blackened one of my eyes and my ribs ached from his kicks. The following day, my sister-in-law kept Katie for me while I went to Bergen to consult an attorney about the possible separation. The attorney listened to me but said he really didn't know what he could do for me because wife beating wasn't grounds for a divorce at that time. I went home feeling so trapped that I sat down and wrote a letter to Mama telling her everything. Before now I always had told her things were all right between us but this time I told her the whole story. I got a letter back right away. She said to let her know when I wanted to come home and she would send me the fare with no questions.

One week after my visit to the attorney my husband received the letter from him. He read it, laughed, and tore it into pieces and burned them, never saying a word about it.

The weeks went by, and he mellowed a little and drank much less. When Katie was about one and a half years old, I became pregnant again, I was happy he had reduced his drinking to next to nothing. Payday came, that's usual, he came home late and, on that evening, particularly drunk. I did not tell him I was pregnant until the next day when he was sober.

Why must you always drink on payday? I asked where the cry was in my voice, then turned them and walked out to the kitchen. Suddenly he was behind me and I felt a solid kick in the small of my back -in the lumbar section!

That is none of your goddamn business, he said suppressing his anger. With that, he went to bed and once again, I went upstairs to my in-laws. While I cried with pain and despair, I told them I was pregnant but probably would lose my baby now. My mother-in-law agreed and shook her head and made me promise to call her if anything started happening to me during the night. The next morning, I got up at the usual time and made him breakfast then he left for work. I felt very tired so I went back to bed. I had been in bed just a little while when I started feeling suspiciously damp. I threw back the covers and saw blood everywhere I found a towel draping myself in it and I called out to my mother-in-law. She came running down and took one look at me, ran to the phone and called the midwife who delivered Katie. The midwife rushed over and examined me. You were in your third month, she said and ordered me to rest in bed for a few days and take the medication she gave me.

That evening my husband was called upstairs to his parents along with his brothers. I don't know what was said but for weeks afterwards, he was the perfect husband. At times he would sit and stare at the floor, then look up at me with an unexplainable expression in his eyes. Many times, I wish that he would talk to me about these inner feelings but he never did. Not long after this happened his grandmother passed away suddenly; her heart just stopped. He was absolutely shattered, and I felt helpless because I had grown to love her as well and she treasured Katie. I sat and watched him drink himself into another stupor of grief, but at least he was home. Neither I nor Katie matter to him right now, only his grief.

Why, Grandma, why did you leave me? He would cry as if he was the only grandchild she had. I thought he sounded so childish, but I didn't say a word unless he spoke first. A week or so after the funeral, he started talking about the ship that he was helping to build. He thought it would be nice to sail with her on her maiden voyage. I began to get excited as well, the thought of sailing and seeing some other countries sounded good, while we were at it, we could build up capital then come home and build a house. We decided to talk things over with my in-laws to see if they would keep Katie while we were sailing. They agreed and we signed on the ship with a 6 months contract. I was so thrilled about this new venture that would give him and me a chance to be alone together for a while and just maybe this would help our relationship which as far as I was concerned, become a little strained.

At this time in Norway, women were taught to honor and stand by their men in marriage no matter what they did to us or how we were treated. I was sad to leave Katie though but she couldn't come with us when we left in May 1957. We sailed from Norway to Germany, where we loaded up with Volkswagens to sell to Newport News Virginia in America. After unloading the cars, we then sailed to Baltimore Maryland to pick up Coal to bring back to Germany. Whenever we were in Port, my husband would get drunk every night and use up all the money he drew out, with all the money I drew out as well. I quickly became aware and wise to his antics and after that didn't draw out much money, I wanted to save for the future. When he discovered this, he became very angry, but I didn't care, I knew he wouldn't dare start anything. I had made a lot of friends on the ship who had told me not to worry that they were on my side.

One evening, we sat in our cabin talking about our family and I was shocked when he suddenly announced that he would have nothing to do with my little daughter at home. I'm not going to raise an illegitimate brat, he announced. This meant that he was going back on the promise that he had made to me before we got married. He had promised me we would bring my daughter to live with us so that she would grow up with our children, when I pointed this out to him, his eyes grew very hard. That's a lie, he said- I never said anything like that!

It was getting close to Christmas, and I wanted to be home with Katie. Anyway, my contract was about to expire and I would not renew even though he had been talking about renewing for himself. I told him I would be going home with or without him and he became very upset over my decision and finally decided to go home.

He was much too jealous to let me travel alone on the long journey home by train from Germany to Norway. It was a beautiful trip through a Wonderland covered with snow. I wanted to experience the trip from Denmark to Sweden because the whole train was ferried across the Strait of Denmark. It was done that night as I slept. We surprised the family by arriving on Christmas Eve. Katie ran into my arms and we clung to each other. Her father wanted to say hello also, so she quickly gave him a hug and a kiss then came back to me and sat on my lap until she fell asleep in my arms much to his jealous mind. Christmas season came and went, and soon it was 1958. I had had a taste of America and couldn't stop thinking or talking about it. Even though I only saw dirty seaports and Port Towns (including the aftermath of a stabbing at the dock in Baltimore). I remembered how open and friendly the people seemed, and how much I liked the atmosphere.

In the flash, I knew what I wanted, I wanted to live in America!! I remembered that my father who passed away, had an aunt who lived in Oregon somewhere, the same who sent the dress I was confirmed in. I wrote my mother and asked for her address and my husband and I composed a letter to her and waited impatiently for a reply. A month, then 2 months went by and finally, we received a letter from her with good news. Yes, she and her husband would be willing to sponsor us! So, from both sides of the ocean, the plan for immigration was set into action. First the immigration office in Oslo, Norway's capital sent us questionnaires with hundreds of items to answer. Then the weight began...

One day, some 10 months later a huge envelope came in the mail. It was our papers!

We sold all our furniture along with the beautiful dishes that we had received as a wedding present from Mama.

I hated to sell those dishes but I was told that everything is so cheap in America, that we could get equally beautiful things once we had been there a while.

Katie was very excited about going up in the air in the big airplane, but she asked me if I was coming along. She didn't worry about her Papa, it's me. I assured her over and over again that I indeed was coming with her. She was a little sad that her Grandma and grandpa weren't coming along, but she assured them that she would come back for them later. My mother-in-law took me aside to speak with me before we left and put her arms around me and cried.' My husband and I have come to know you very well and we love you beyond anything else, and you and Katie are very special to us. But listen, Randi, since you are not able to get a divorce here, but you will be able to do that, where you're going. The law will protect you from harm there and you will have a new life ahead of you. Live, girl, live!' I started crying as well, it must have been hard for her to make this speech since this wasn't her normal way of talking, she was never soft like this. My father in-law was holding Katie, she had been the apple of his eye ever since she was born.

"My Katie, my Katie, I love you so," he crooned with a voice that wasn't quite steady as he sat rocking my girl back and forth. My husband on the other hand had no remorse; he just stood there with a huge hangover. The night before he had been in town saying goodbye to his friends and came home drunk as usual, but I didn't care anymore. While we stood there waiting to board the plane, my mind wandered up north to my family. Katie and I made the trip there during the summer while we still were waiting for the immigration papers to arrive. This was the first time Evy had seen Katie and they became good friends. When Katie came to sit on my lap, Evy would sit on my other knee and I basked in happiness- imagine my two girls together! I wish that it could stay like this, but I knew it wouldn't as long as I stayed married to him. Mama and I had a lot of good talks while I was visiting; as long as you and your husband live in Norway, you can always come home if something happens between you two you know that, Randi? But once you move to America, you'll be on your own; mama warned. When Katie and I left my hometown, it was extremely difficult to say goodbye. But the most difficult thing I had to do by far was leaving Evy behind! When I had left her the first time to go to work it hadn't been as bad because I knew I would see her again. But this time I didn't know when, if ever, I would see her again. As I held that little skinny body of hers close to mine, she clung to me very hard and didn't say a word which was very typical of her to do. During the two weeks Katie and I had visited, Evy didn't say much of anything, Katie wants to Chatterbox. But I would catch her there staring at me with those beautiful blue eyes of hers. When she discovered that I was looking back at her, she would squirm, look down, and smile with embarrassment. At those times I wanted to take her in my arms and never let her go!

Then that would be returned to Reality by a tugging at my arm, it would be Katie, looking into my eyes with a questioning look. So, I would bend down and give her a hug, then invite Evy to join in and she didn't have to be asked twice, there we all would stand hugging each other and laughing. Sometimes I would catch Mama's eyes filling up with tears and she would only smile.

The three of you have something special going between you and there is a bond being formed that will never be broken," Mama would say.

Papa would take both girls for a walk, one on each hand. The girls had a lot of fun talking about what he said. When we first arrived, my brother thought it was fun, and he soon felt outnumbered by those two, meaning the girls. He would Retreat to play games with his friends but that didn't matter much to the girls they had each other and their own games.

Then came the day when we had to say goodbye. Evy stood and nervously fingered the pockets on her pinafore. I opened my arms and she practically jumped into them and locked her arms around my neck whispering in my ear;" I love you, Mama". "You are my special girl and always will be. I love you a lot," I whispered back. When I put her back down on the ground, she had a smile on her face and I felt uplifted, not quite so sad anymore as I felt I had done the right thing.

Suddenly I was rocked back to reality as the plane was ready to board. It was hard to say our final goodbyes to my in-law's family, through good and bad, for nearly 4 years. Now I would be on my own, would have no one! The plane took off for our new land and we settled down for 17 hours in the air. After an hour or so, Katie wanted to walk around and the flight attendant came and took her back to the kitchen, where she gave Katie a soft drink. Katie came back and told us all about her walk and how nice the lady was. For some reason, my husband didn't say much during the trip but ordered the beer for himself, sat down, and took a nap never bothering with the care of Katie. I felt this if there were two voices inside of me arguing... What is your fascination with this Lush of a man? One voice would ask. But you love him! said Voice number two. But is he true to you or does he cheat? The first voice wants to know.

A while before we left Norway, I had heard that he had been in the company of a young lady on one who nightly escapades. When I confronted him about it, he got angry and demanded to know who had said this, but I refused to tell him. Deep in my heart, I knew this person spoke the truth, especially since a family member had tipped me off. Why would this person try to break up my little family and put the rest of the family at odds with a lie?

Katie stirred in my arms, trying to change to a more comfortable position. I wondered why he couldn't cuddle and hug his daughter. At times, she wanted so badly to sit on his lap but he never seemed to notice this. It was a rare occasion when he would go for a walk with her. In fact, I could count on one hand the times he had done so. What would the future hold for my family? I wondered. Would I be left alone in a strange country if he decided to leave me? Thoughts whirled- through my mind's corridors like snowflakes in the Wind.

Suddenly Katie jerked herself awake and looked at me with Wild eyes. Oh, mama, I'm glad you are here because I saw the plane go up in the air, I was on the plane with Papa and you stood on the ground! She was shaking with fear. I hugged her tightly and soon she settled down again. My husband slept all the way to our first stop, London. We had that 3-hour layover there, but we didn't dare go very far, so we walked around the airport and Window Shopped. Finally, we boarded the plane for the final leg of our journey, the longest and most boring. The plane would land briefly somewhere in Canada to refuel, then off to Seattle, and finally end up in Portland Oregon, our destination.

It was evening when we boarded another plane in London. We were served supper as soon as the plane was in the air. After we ate, I realized how terribly exhausted I was and how I needed to sleep, so he reluctantly took Katie on his lap. The flight attendant gave Katie a few things to play with, since the two seats ahead of us were empty they were turned into a playpen. Katie was delighted, and I was able to sleep. After 2 and 1/2 hours, I walk as suddenly as if somebody has shaken me. I looked around but didn't see him anywhere, Katie was still playing on the seats in front of us, but where was my husband? When a flight attendant came by, I asked her about him. I think he's found someone in the back of the plane to talk to. When I went back there and found him having drinks with some people, I was so disgusted that I wanted to cry. Is this the way it's going to be in our new land? I thought that I returned back to my seat. Soon it was announced that we were about to land in Canada. All the passengers would have to leave the plane while the refueling took place. I had to wake Katie and take her on my lap, but she didn't protest. When we stepped off the plane in Canada it was bitterly cold and the snow was falling. We all huddled together in the waiting room until we could be re-boarded. When we arrived in Seattle, we had to go to the immigration office, which I thought was scary. Then we changed planes again and were off to Portland. Somewhere between Seattle and Portland, my feet started to swell, but I didn't dare take my shoes off because I knew I wouldn't be able to put them back on again. The swelling came from sitting still and from the change of climate.

My aunt and uncle met us at the Portland airport. She was happy to see us, but her husband was very reserved in his actions. I didn't speak more than a couple of words in English and my husband would keep the conversation going fairly well with his English. The 3-hour-drive from Portland to their family farm seemed long and I was near exhaustion when we finally arrived. Katie slept most of the way. I fell in love with their Farm which was located just a few miles outside of Winston Oregon and covered around 100 acres with 50 cattle, a few ducks and cats, and the cocker spaniel named Grumpy who took to Katie right away and followed her everywhere. The farm was located in a lovely clearing. I love The Heat of Summer but I didn't eat much so I lost a lot of weight at first. My aunt worried about me and thought I was homesick, even though I assured her that that wasn't the case, deep down inside I knew she was right not only did I miss Evy terribly, but I also miss speaking Norwegian and hearing it spoken all the time. Lots of times I would go out in the field, sit down on the stump, and cry until I had no more tears left. Then I would go down to the creek that trickled past the back of the house, wash my face and, sit and watch The Little Creatures going about their daily chores. The Ducks were so tame that they would come up close to me as long as Grumpy wasn't around. As far as immigration was concerned Uncle Jay told them that we were hired to work on his farm. My husband did, but it actually turned out to be all work until our tickets were paid. My husband worked with Jay on his logging operation in the woods while I stayed around the farm with my aunt and Katie. Since my aunt didn't drive, we were stuck there except for weekly shopping trips to Roseburg on Saturdays.

After 9 months in the US, we were still at the farm with another cent in our pockets. He had been a real husband to me during all those months, so I relaxed and felt at ease.

I noticed that he was becoming increasingly restless and started talking about getting out on his own. At first, my aunt and her husband were against it and why shouldn't they be -they had help they didn't have to pay a cent in wages to! We decided that they couldn't hold on to us and moved to Winston. Our landlady, Mrs. Hahn became my good friend. One day she asked if I would like to learn more English so I could at least go shopping alone. I thought that it made good sense.

I didn't tell my husband because I knew he would be against it. In his mind, he figured that if I learned enough English, I would speak with people meaning men at the stores. The men would then become interested in me because of my accent, leaving him to fend them off! What he really wanted was to have total control over me! He said 'that a wife should stay home while the man worked and when he came home, she should have his food ready'! I thought all that was pure nonsense! After we had been living in town for a couple of weeks, he discovered the tavern. I became very nervous and that funny feeling returned to the pit of my stomach. I became very watchful so Mrs. Hahn wouldn't find out about his problem. Since there were no buses in town, he decided that we needed a car. Jay, my aunt's husband, co-signed the contract, but he refused to teach me to drive because that would mean that he could keep fewer tabs on me! As the weeks went by, my English got better and better, but although speaking everyday English was one thing, writing was quite another! Even Einar had trouble with writing English.

One day he decided to buy a used TV from an advertisement in the newspaper. The man who was selling the TV was an attorney who drew up his own sales contract. I took an instant liking to him and his family, but Einar wasn't interested. Although I couldn't figure out why not- I didn't push it with his temper, I knew better.

Chapter 7

We had lived in Winston for a few weeks when one day Mrs. Hahn asked if I would like to earn some money for myself. I became excited about the project but said that I'd have to discuss it with my husband first. She looked at me but didn't comment and continued to say that a friend of hers needed a babysitter for a few hours during the day and I could bring Katie along to play with her little girl!

When I spoke with Einar about it, he was surprised at the thought I even considered it, thinking I didn't know very much English.

"I've learned a few sentences," I said and let it go at that.

"I guess it's all right for you to work then," he said.

Mrs. McIntosh, my new employer, picked me up at 7;30 every morning and Einar would come and take me home. He wanted my earnings at his disposal but I said I was using it on groceries when in reality, I was hiding it away.

I wrote to Mama often and told her that if she needed to write something special-for my eyes, only she was to send it to Mrs. Hahn, that way Einar couldn't get a hold of it and she was happy to be the 'go-between' as she had 'guessed' what was going on! He often commented on all the food in the house and asked if I had been shopping alone.

"With Mrs. Hahn's help," I answered. This way I didn't really lie, she had helped me!

One Saturday afternoon, a salesman showed up at the door and since Einar was home, we invited him in. We chatted for a while and the man told us that his and his wife's parents came from Norway and right away the three of us felt a 'kin-ship' with each other! He didn't make a sale but we formed a friendship bond and each time he came to town, he would stop by for a cup of coffee!

One time when Bob came and had lunch with us, Einar had made his decision that he wanted to sell albums for Bob's company!

Unfortunately, this company was located in Medford, which meant that we had to move again! I had reservations about quitting my job and moving away from the only good friend I had, Mrs. Hahn! We had been living in Winston for only 10 months. And I had worked only 3 mo. This meant we would have to write Immigration and inform them of our move. If we didn't write, we risked deportation with 'no questions asked'!

We did move, however, and found the cutest older apartment and settled in.

Einar started working for Bob as an apprentice, then actually started selling these albums on his own and he traveled throughout southern Oregon and northern California. Soon he discovered that there was not much money to be made and he missed not being able to come home at the end of the day!

By this time, he was also used to speaking English. Our relationship had stabilized to a point, where he wasn't drinking as much, and only when we visited Bob and Marna, the salesman, and his wife. Soon, I found I was pregnant again, and thinking back to my last pregnancy when he kicked me, I lost the baby and hoped to carry this to full term. One day we saw an advertisement in the paper that intrigued us. A lady wanted a caretaker for her place and would accept a family with one child. We drove to her place and applied for the job. Her place was lovely with trees all around and tall mountains towering above it all and the Klamath River flowed lazily by her property! The houses were painted white with blue trim, as were the guest cottages. There was a sunken garden with dozens of rose bushes, hibiscus, and other flowers that seemed to try to outdo each other with their blooms and fragrances. Towering above the flowers were luscious fruit trees!

The guest cottages were used during the summer months, when friends of Mrs. Martha (as she liked to be called), would arrive to stay and do fishing in the river. We were hired and moved into the caretaker's cottage. It was small but very pretty and we didn't need much room. There was a tiny kitchen, a pantry, a bathroom, and a combination bedroom/sitting room. Nothing was painted, all was varnished natural wood. In one kitchen corner, stood a huge, old floor model radio. Sometimes we could get a Medford radio station but since we lived in between tall mountains and had no antennas, reception was extremely poor.

Soon after we arrived, I began baking bread and proudly gave a loaf to Mrs. Martha.

She, in turn, suggested I'd bake and sell to her friends during the summer to earn pocket money, which I did! Since we had no rent or utility bills, our salary was ours to keep. One day I thought of the TV set we had left with Bob and Marna in Medford and wished we could have it with us but I knew the signal would not carry through the mountains. I suddenly thought of the contract of sale and asked 'if he had paid it off?'

"Yes, a long time ago!" he assured me.

Since he never let me handle anything that had to do with household money, I believed him. Soon I started to reveal my pregnancy and thought I'd better tell Mrs. Martha about my condition. When I did, she looked at me with those mild eyes of hers and said; "I knew you were pregnant when you applied for the job!"

As I sat there looking at her in surprise, I thought how much I had grown to like this short, slightly overweight woman who had curly grey hair and glasses. She has a gentle voice that would become very sharp when she was agitated and when she was angry, the voice almost went silent. Summer turned into fall and I felt happy and relaxed at the prospect of a baby coming into our lives. At the end of Oct. Mrs. Martha said she was leaving to spend the winter months in her home in Fresno. This would leave us with almost nothing to do except for a few repair jobs for him to do. I was all right by myself, I didn't feel like doing anything anyway because the baby was due sometime toward the end of November. Einar had been drinking very little, only an occasional beer at home and I was joyous. We made friends with our neighbors, a young couple the same age as us. Bill and Kathy had a son Allen, who was quite a bit younger than Katie. The two rarely played together because Allen was extremely possessive about his toys.

Bill worked as a prison guard at a work camp a few miles down the valley and Kathy was a 'stay-at-home mom' like me. Kathy and I spent a lot of time together and did a lot of 'girl-talking'. She and Bill still acted like 'newlywed' and I was a bit envious because every time I touched Einar or kissed him, he wanted sex. I refused because I worried about the unborn baby, he became sullen and would pout for hours.

I longed to be held by him but that he wanted no part of- period!

Sometimes when I was resting, Katie would come and lay down beside me and put her ear on my stomach, patting gently and whispering; "Don't worry baby, I will take care of you after you are born." Then with a smile, she would look at me with those big, blue eyes and I would melt.

"Does the baby hurt you sometimes?" she would ask solemnly.

"Yes, when he kicks me."

She thought for a moment, and then she said, "That's because he's running out of room, right?" I would give her a hug and soon we both went to sleep.

As the year was coming to a close, we were getting winter weather with cold winds and black ice on the roads and I worried constantly because the hospital was some 1 ½ hour drive on good roads. Then one day I felt uneasy and had no appetite and around bedtime, the pains started and I alerted Einar. He quickly made a bed for Katie in the back seat of the car, grabbed my suitcase and we were off toward the hospital! The icy roads scared me so much that the pains became very dull, but I didn't say a word to him about it though because he might have thought that the pains were false labor. We spent the better of 3 hours.

I was wheeled in and the doctor asked him to wait while I was examined and he was told that the baby was on its way. One of the nurses had made a makeshift bed for Katie in one of the rooms and Einar sat there with her so she wouldn't get scared and 15 min later on December 9th,1962, John was born.

With his black hair and tiny body, John was so beautiful that I couldn't take my eyes off him! None of my children had been large in size when born and John was no different but he had a set of lungs on him that he used to let us know he had arrived!! As soon as Einar heard that he had a son and everything was all right, he gathered up Katie, who had slept through the whole ordeal and drove home.

Since I lived so far away from the hospital, I stayed one week because the doctor wanted to make sure that there were no complications before he released me to go home with my bundle of joy. Einar and Katie were to pick me up on the day of my release. I was dressed and had John dressed as well for travel when they arrived.

Katie opened his wrap, touched his cheek with her finger and with a sparkle in her eyes said; "Thank you, mama, for bringing him to me, he is beautiful!"

I felt so touched that I started to cry but my husband just stood there, saying and doing nothing. The lady in the bed next to mine had tears in her eyes as she said;" what lovely children you have I thanked her and said my 'goodbyes'. While we were on the road toward home, Katie reached over my shoulder and touched her brother's hand.

"I love you mama and my baby brother, too'! I kissed her hand and smiled back. The weeks went by and slowly I gained my strength back. Since I gave birth, he had not been drinking and I felt as if we were becoming a 'real family'! He had even stopped nagging Katie at the table like he used to for being such a slow eater.

She would pick at her food and that irritated Einar immensely. I thought it was just a phase she was going through and that she would grow out of, and since she was otherwise healthy, I didn't worry too much!

Spring came and Mrs. Martha came back. When she saw John, she fell in love with him. She enjoyed watching Katie display the deep caring she had for her little brother." There's a bond between those two that will last forever"! Mrs. Martha said.

My happiness was not to last, for he started visiting taverns again. He'd stop by on the way home from grocery shopping trips. At first, I thought; 'Well let him it's alright'! Then it started happening about once a week when he would stay out all evening and most of the night. I was getting that 'old feeling' in the pit of my stomach.

One Sunday he drove off at about 2:00 in the afternoon and didn't come home until 9;00 that evening. I saw he was drunk when he walked in the door. Right away he wanted me to serve him dinner.

"We ate hours ago, Einar," I told him. "There's a bowl of stew on the counter for you." With that, I turned to tend to the baby, who had been awakened by his loud voice. As I walked past Einar, he whirled and kicked me in the small of my back. I never said a word but something inside of me changed. I knew then that I had to do something about the situation and started working on a plan.

Spring turned into early summer and that brought the guests from California. When Mar. Martha handed us our paycheck, he said he'd go to Happy Camp to cash the check and pick up groceries. I didn't see him again until the next morning around 7:30ish. This is it, I thought, I've had enough! When he walked in and flopped on the couch, I was sitting eating breakfast with Katie. I didn't say a word for fear my voice wouldn't carry. Finally, he spoke; "Aren't you going to say anything or at least fix my breakfast?"

For the first time in our marriage, I looked at this extremely handsome man with disgust. I lit a cigarette with hands that didn't shake- to my amazement- and spoke slowly and calmly.

"This time you have gone too far, Einar. Our marriage is finished. I want you out of my life and out of this place by twelve noon!"

He jumped off the couch as if something had kicked him and asked me to repeat what I had said while he slowly walked toward me. I went cold all over and grabbed the kitchen knife.

"One step closer and you have had it!" I warned in the same calm voice.

He stopped and backed up a step, staring at me in disbelief- never taking his eyes off me, he backed up all the way back to the couch. I felt strange but good while I kept wondering where that calmness came from. What would happen next?

I glanced at Katie and saw she was still eating. Because of my calm voice, she had not become upset at all, in fact, it didn't even seem as if she had been listening! Imagine! I stood up to him and he backed down!

He slumped on the couch again. I looked out the window and saw Mrs. Martha coming up the walk, knocking once, and entering the kitchen.

"Good morning, all!" she greeted. Then she turned to Einar and said, "It's time for work, are you coming today?"

"In about an hour, He said," I just came home."

'No Einar," she said, winking at me." YOU WILL BE ON THE JOB WITHIN THE HOUR OR LEAVE THE PREMISES! YOU HAVE 1 HOUR!"

He still lay on the couch, either in defiance or maybe shock.

I calmly went to the bedroom and got his suitcase which I had already packed the night before and carried it to the couch and dropped it by his side.

"I want the leftover money from the check and the groceries!" I snapped.

"There's only three dollars left from the check and no groceries at all!" he sneered.

"Alright," I answered, "Take your bag and leave. I don't want to see you again. As I said, you have until noon!"

John awoke just then, wanting breakfast and a diaper change and I gladly obliged so My mind could be directed to my children and not him! Katie instinctively knew what was going on, I think because she didn't look nor speak to her father.

While I was feeding her brother his bottle, she stood beside us, kissing his hand and my arm. When John was done eating, I took both children and walked down to Mrs. Martha, where I knew I'd be safe from his possible rage!

A while later, there was a knock at the front door- it was him, he wanted to speak with me! "What do you want?" I asked.

"I just wanted to speak with you," he said quietly.

"We have nothing to talk about, Einar- all has been said before!"

I knew that I had the upper hand, I couldn't tell what he was thinking but his tears were either from exhaustion or his hangover plus the realization that he would have a long drive ahead of him. But I had ceased to care, I was in limbo and didn't feel anything.

"Goodbye Einar," I said and closed the door quietly.

After he'd gone, I realized that he had not said 'goodbye' to his children, especially Katie, who was old enough to notice what was going on but not understand the outcome. It made me cold with anger- Imagine, his own children!

That very evening, the phone rang at Mrs. Martha- someone wanted to speak with me. It was our mutual 'friend' Bob from Medford. Einar had gone to them and now Bob was pleading with me to take him back and that Einar was 'really suffering'!

I listened calmly then replied: "It's none of your business Bob!" and hung up the phone. He must have told them a 'whopper' of a story because I didn't hear from them until a year later.

After he had gone, the days floated by slowly. I cried a lot, slept very little, and lost a lot of weight because food didn't taste good. Now and again, Katie would ask when Papa would come back and say 'hello'. I tried to explain as much as I thought she could understand.

At that time a man and his wife who used to be caretakers for the place, arrived to spend their vacation there. The woman Hazel, took over my daily chores and also took care of both me and the children. I felt as if I was living a dream, nothing seemed real to me. Hazel asked if I would like to come with them to Fresno and I gladly accepted the offer, anything to add distance between him and myself. I thought of the Immigration and moving and talked to Mrs. Martha who said her brother-in-law would take care of that and that he was an attorney.

Hazel and her husband Forrest, spent their vacation helping to do Einar's chores and 'catch-up' work. Sometimes Hazel would try coaxing me to talk about my relationship saying;" You will feel better if you get it out in the open," she said and I discovered she was right!

She helped me pack my belongings, and we left with them to go to Fresno where I hoped he wouldn't find us. Mrs. Martha promised she wouldn't reveal anything.

When we arrived in Fresno, I thought it was extremely hot there but Forrest said I'd get used to it, which I did! Hazel said that we would stay with friends of Mrs. Martha who were very nice and when they dropped us off, we were given lots of hugs before they drove off to their home somewhere in Southern California.

I felt very uncomfortable being in a situation where I had to depend on other people and many a night, I cried myself to sleep from despair and loneliness. I wished that I could fly back to Norway and my family, but I knew there was no chance of that!

I remembered Mrs. Martha's brother-in-law, the attorney who held very high standards in the Fresno court system, I had heard said and thought I'd ask his advice. He checked with Immigration who said that they never gave out any information such as mine unless it was of a criminal nature and even then, it had to be investigated first. Was I ever happy to hear that!!! I knew I was safe and felt a little lighter at heart and body. I stayed with my new family for 3 months, and I felt so lost the entire time. I didn't know anybody in the town and I also longed to be with my own kind. In particular, I was so tired of speaking English and wanted to speak my own language again. I started to think about Aunt Aslaug, but I was so unsure of what to do. Here I was, forced to think for myself, making huge decisions in which I had to be careful not to mess up the immediate future for me and my children and I didn't know where to start! Einar had never allowed me to think for myself and make my own decisions. Going against my deep feelings, I wrote a letter to my aunt, telling her about my situation. I received a return back with money for a bus ticket from Fresno to Roseburg, Oregon where she and her husband would pick us up at the station. Before I left Fresno, I stayed a day with Mrs. Martha, to say my 'good-bye' and 'thank you' to her and her kind heart. She then said that she had paid for my 'room & board' at the Fletts!

I started crying as I said: "I have no way of paying you back"

She hugged me and said: "It's alright, you're just like a daughter to me!"

The trip back to Oregon was long and tiring for both me and the children. John slept most of the way, only waking long enough for a change of diapers and something to eat. Katie played with her doll and a basket she used as a doll bed.

Chapter 8

The driver allowed her to walk around a little bit and talk with the passengers and since she didn't speak much English, they thought she was fun to listen to!

One lady I guessed was in her sixties also bound for Roseburg, took it upon herself to offer her help with the children, so I could get some rest. She put Katie in the seat beside her while she held John and I got a little sleep. It felt good to rest!

After a short nap, I awoke with a panicked jerk, wondering where my children were, only to find Katie fast asleep next to this lady and John being gently rocked on her lap all the while she sat with closed eyes and a smile on her lips, humming a tune to herself. When the bus would make a stop, she would grab the children and ask me to come along to the cafe for something to eat and she would always pay for the food. When I protested and wanted to pay her back, she would just shake her head. "Tsk, tsk," she would say, "You have already paid me back by easing my trip and letting me tend to your precious children!"

"Do you have children of your own?" I asked very carefully.

She looked down at my boy sleeping in her arms and nodded.

She then told me a tale of horror.

She had six children but lost them all in a fire where her house burned down to the ground, along with her husband who had gone to try to save them. As she spoke, tears were streaming down her face. I felt tears stinging my eyes and running down my cheeks as well and I didn't know what to say and kept quiet.

Katie opened her eyes and looked from me to the woman but kept still. After a while, she sat up and touched the woman's hand and broke the silence…

"You can play with me and hold my brother all you want, mama won't mind, will you mama?" she asked.

"Of course, my love," I answered.

Finally, we arrived in Roseburg. I was so happy to see my aunt that I fell into her arms crying. Katie tugged at my dress while she looked searchingly through the crowd and said;" Where did that nice grandma from the bus go, Mama?"

I searched as well but she was nowhere to be seen and said;" She probably went home." Katie's unsmiling eyes looked at me and she said;" Don't you remember Mama, she said she had no home!" "No," I answered, "she said that she had no children".

"Isn't that the same thing, mama?" I must have looked like I fell from the sky and glanced at my aunt who was dabbing her eyes.

"Yes, it is the same, dear."

Katie enjoyed being on the farm again. Grumpy the dog was visibly happy to see her but my aunt was worried about me. "You have lost too much weight," she said, "I'm going to have to do something about that!"

My aunt really enjoyed John- he was a good baby who never cried much. She had two sons of her own so this to her was refreshing. I busied myself with work around the house. It felt good to be doing something that I found myself humming a tune, which I hadn't done in a long time. I also thought a lot about my failed marriage.

In his own warped way, he must have loved me once, because there were times when he spoke so softly and was so tender. Those were the times that I cherish the most. As I thought back to the time after John was born, those good times could be counted on one hand. Why? I really wondered. Did he find someone else?

But now- I wasn't going to work myself up into an anguish about the past, I resolved. I let it go and threw myself into work at the ranch. But no matter how much I had to do or how nice my aunt and Jay were to us, with nobody my own age to talk to, I felt trapped and lonely. I started thinking about earning money to support myself but with two small children, a little training in restaurant work from my youth in Norway, and a language barrier to overcome?

My aunt and Jay got a little help from the state to support the kids and me, but it just covered the food. Then something else happened that threw me into a new despair again! One day Jay asked me if I would like to come along to town for a few errands he had to do. I jumped at the chance to get away for a while and my aunt offered to watch the children. On the way back Jay stopped the truck and started touching me and saying how much he would like to go to bed with me.

"Take your hands off me and never touch me again!" I said coldly. "Start this truck and take me back to the farm immediately!"

Jay pleaded with me not to tell my aunt and I promised that I wouldn't.

"I'm not stupid!" I spoke.

Once again, I turned to Mrs. Martha for advice. I got a letter back right away with a suggestion. She knew of a family who wanted to adopt one or two children from the same family. For several weeks I tumbled with this idea and then I talked to my aunt who thought it was a splendid idea.

"You are much too young to be stuck here at the farm with the children," she said. "You could be in town earning money and living your own life."

I wrote back to Mrs. Martha and agreed to let the couple meet Katie and John.

Not long after, they arrived in Roseburg and I really enjoyed seeing Mrs. Martha again. Mr. And Mrs. Griffith were very nice people from Fresno CA. He was tall and had a nice open smile. She had a gentle mannerism that fascinated me. They had brought along their own daughter, who had straight blond hair fastened with a bow.

Mrs. Griffith told me they had only one child because she could not have any more for medical reasons. They wanted two more at least and my children would be perfect! They thought John was an absolute 'doll' and John in turn, really put on a show. He was 9 months old with blond hair like his father and the same blue eyes and he cooed and giggled to anyone who spoke to him. Katie was another matter; she would not leave my side but just stood there holding onto my dress and staring with those big eyes of hers. The Griffiths wanted to take John with them when they left on that day. I knew the inevitable day had come, so I consented. Tears flowed down my face while I packed his belongings. When Katie came into the bedroom, I sat down on the bed and let her climb into my lap. She dried my tears and looked searchingly into my eyes while she cupped her hands around my face;" Don't worry mama, we will get John back again," she said softly.

We picked up John's things and carried them out to the living room. I picked him up to say 'goodbye' but all I could do was kiss him. Then I bent down to Katie so she could kiss her brother.

"I love you John, and Mama does too," she said, "We'll see you soon."

After Mrs. Martha and the Griffiths left Katie and I took a walk out in the field.

I sat down on my usual tree stump and let the tears flow. Katie kissed my cheeks and put her little arms around my neck.

"Don't be sad, mama," she said in a voice that wasn't too steady. "We'll see John again soon." I sat her on my lap and held her tight.

"You will see John soon, dear," I told her. She jumped off my lap and said:" Let's run in the field, mama!" We ran and played until both of us were exhausted and thirsty. Then we ran to the creek, lay on our stomachs, and drank fresh, cool water. We sat and watched the water trickle over the rocks for a while, then Katie turned to me and with almost a grown-up confidence said:" Mama, I have been thinking. I know you love John and John loves you back and Papa does not love us. Now it is only us girls left so we must work hard so Papa will never find us ever again!"

I could not believe those words came from a four-year-old child. "You're right, Katie," I nodded.

My aunt remembered a friend of hers who was a deputy sheriff and he and his wife had met Katie on a few occasions while visiting the farm and they liked her right away. When they heard about my situation, they offered to help by having Katie come and stay with them until I could make other arrangements for her. They invited us to visit their little farm and Katie liked the place right away. They had two boys, one Katie's age and the other, a couple of years older. She wanted to stay with them as much as they wanted her to stay which made me feel good!

There was only one thing bothering me -it was her language barrier.

For the most part, she had been around me and we didn't bother. Frankly, I hadn't thought of it being really important. She knew some but could not say full sentences yet. I talked it over with the woman and she promised me that she would take it slowly. So, I left her there and moved to Roseburg. When I said my 'goodbye', her parting words were; "Remember mama, we have to work hard, really hard!"

I knew she had been thinking of the conversation she and I had at the creek. I found a job as a waitress and my working hours were mainly evenings so the days were my own. Since I didn't drive and depended on others, I rarely saw Katie. I had to rely on others to bring her to me and that didn't happen very often.

Every time I saw her, I had this gnawing feeling that all was not well between her and the Reynolds. One might call that a 'mother's intuition'. She wasn't allowed to stay long, maybe ½ hr. at the most. I began to wonder if they were afraid of something that she might say that she wasn't supposed to mention. I also noticed that my girl was not the 'happy fun-loving' girl that was mine, anymore. Why?

Since I couldn't figure it out, I attributed my feelings to my imagination which was playing tricks on me! The Reynolds were Christian people who went to church every Sunday. What could possibly be wrong?

Every time Katie left, I felt terribly lonely and empty inside. In a few short months, I had gone from a family of 4 to a family of 1, with no one to worry and fuss over except myself!

My apartment was across the street from a restaurant and bar that I started frequenting for something to do. If I stayed at home, I'd just sit and smoke one cigarette after the other followed by cups of coffee as well. Sometimes my loneliness was so bad that I caught myself wishing I had Einar by my side again and I knew that those were moments of 'desperation'!

At the restaurant and bar, I befriended the barmaid, Candy, who opened up and said that she was divorced and her husband had taken off with their child. The police had been looking for them for quite some time.

Candy and I started hanging out together on our days off. Since she had a car, we went on drives which I enjoyed. I also opened up to her and shared about my family life and Katie and who she was staying with.

"Let's go to visit her sometime," Candy suggested one day.

On several occasions, we drove to the ranch but no one was there and for some reason, it bothered me! I tried calling the ranch but whoever answered would rarely allow her to speak with me. When I did have a chance, she would just speak a couple of words, then she would hang up the phone. I shared my fears with Candy, who became thoughtful, but concluded there probably wasn't anything to worry about.

Weeks passed by and I learned to live without my precious girl, that is not get to see her for weeks at a time.

One day I was window shopping downtown when I felt a light tap on my shoulder and a 'Hi Randi'! There stood the attorney who Einar bought the TV from. He bought a cup of coffee for us at a coffee shop and we sat and talked about what had happened since we saw each other last.

"By the way, did you receive all of our TV payments?" I wanted to know.

"No, only two of them," he replied. That surprised me, yet it didn't.

"What do you think we should do about it?" he asked.

"I think he should pay his debts," I said.

"I agree, I'll start the process!"

I didn't hear anything more about it until a couple of weeks later when there was a knock on my door. There stood the attorney, all smiles with the news that the authorities had found Einar in Coos Bay. They brought him to Roseburg and put him in jail to await his trial.

I still to this day don't know how he found out that I lived in Roseburg. The attorney swore on the Bible that he had said nothing about me or my whereabouts to anyone. I received a message from Einar- could I come to see him? He wanted to talk about something important. So silly me, I went to see him! He hadn't changed at all, still the handsome, blue-eyed man I used to know. The 'important thing' he wanted to talk to me about was that he wanted to know if he could go to bed with me or not! "I need you!" he pleaded.

But something had happened to me during all those months apart… I discovered I didn't need him anymore. The 'magic' I used to feel when I was near him had disappeared and I was free! I could only stand to spend about 15 minutes and when I walked outside, I took a deep breath, held my head high, and vowed not to visit that place ever again! I felt so good that I started humming a tune to myself! When I thought back at our conversation at the jail, something dawned on me. He never asked about his children! I didn't say a word about them either. He sure cared about the children he fathered; I thought in anger. I let Mrs. Martha know when the trial was to take place.

One day Mrs. Martha, her sister, and brother-in-law the attorney came from Fresno, to be by my side to support me in case the court wanted me to testify. Our so-called mutual friends from Medford,

Bob, and Marna showed up on Einar's behalf and refused to speak to me. We all stood in the hallway outside of the courtroom, and only my 'true 'friends from Fresno talked to me!

The door from the jail opened and Einar and his court-appointed attorney walked into the hallway. Einar walked over to me and started speaking in Norwegian to me while trying to put his arm around my waist!

I wriggled out of his grip and told him, in English, that I was not interested in speaking Norwegian! It was a lie but what else could I have done?

While I spoke, I looked him straight in the eyes.

It felt so good to see him back away that I was speechless! His attorney made some remark about us getting cozy and chummy, but I didn't bother to reply, I just gave him a cold stare!

A couple of weeks before the trial I had found out from Mr. Reynolds that my aunt and Jay were very angry that I didn't stay at the farm and work for them. I could not understand this because it was my aunt who had suggested that I should move to town and work. What was this sudden turnabout?

As for the advances from Jay, I never told her anything- after all, she's my grandfather's sister and my family. I couldn't put her through that, I loved her and had since the first time I laid my eyes on her. From where I sat in the court, I would catch Jay staring at me, undressing me with his eyes, while my aunt gave me cold stares. When the court session was over, I walked across the floor to my aunt and Jay shook hands with them both and thanked them for what they had done for me.

Jay's mouth opened in surprise and My aunt had tears in her eyes. That was the last time I saw either one of them.

Einar received a six-month sentence. When I asked the immigration authorities about that, they said he should have been deported, so I talked with the judge who had sentenced him.

"Why didn't you deport Einar?" I asked.

"I didn't have the heart to do that." He spoke.

I pointed out to the judge that by letting him stay, I put my life in danger. He thought I was joking. Letters started coming from the jail, uncensored because they were smuggled out but I brought them to the judge right away. I also received a hand-delivered note stuck with tape on my front door. I knew that Einar knew where I lived and he had someone watching my every move and my place!

Candy and I discovered that one night after we closed up the bar and were walking home. Since we lived on the same street, just four houses apart, Candy would walk me home and then go to her own place. One night we saw a car parked on our street with a person seated behind the wheel and the headlights were turned off. Candy asked me to come and sleep at her place that night. The next day, my attorney and I went to the judge and told him about all the strange things that had been happening to me of late. The judge wrote a warrant that I was to carry on my person for the next 5 years! The warrant entitled me to call the police if Einar or any of his so-called friends approached me in any way that was threatening. They could be imprisoned without question if they tried anything!

A couple of weeks later, the authorities moved him to a big prison in Portland. I heard word that he had become too difficult to handle in Roseburg's little jail.

I celebrated Christmas of 1962 with Candy and her friends. It was a sad and lonely day for me. I didn't get a hold of Katie. I tried calling but there was no answer and no one contacted me either from there. I spent New Year's Eve alone, crying myself asleep. After Einar had served five months of his sentence, I received news that he would be released. I became worried about Katie and of course myself.

I phoned Mrs. Martha and she arranged for us to be picked up the following week-end by her, her sister Nell, and brother -in-law the attorney. I sent word to Reynolds that I would be picking Katie up. I worked up to the last day just in case there was someone still watching me. I didn't want to arouse suspicion, so I packed behind closed drapes. Mrs. Martha and her family picked me up. We had lunch at a cafe, and then we drove to the ranch to pick Katie up. When we arrived at the farmhouse, we didn't see Katie anywhere. Mrs. Reynolds, a little woman with piercing dark eyes, answered the door.

"I have come for Katie," I said.

"Katie's in her bedroom," she replied in a sharp tone as she pointed at the closed door I walked in and found Katie sitting on the bed with her legs crossed in Indian fashion. She looked white as a sheet and to me, looked scared to death!

"What's wrong, Katie?" I asked gently. Katie didn't answer or speak at all. Her eyes were huge with fear and she moved slowly like a caged animal.

I turned to Mrs. Reynolds and demanded an explanation. She was calm when she told us that she and her husband had been sitting up all night several nights in a row, trying to turn Katie into a Christian child so that God would receive her." But Katie wouldn't!" the woman said and threw up her hands in disappointment.

By this time, I was really angry at myself for not having seen what was going on before now! I wanted to tell the woman what she could do with her religion, but no words came.

Then, in a low and calm voice from anger I'm sure, Mrs. Martha asked me to take Katie out to the car, while she stayed behind for a short moment.

I sat down in the back seat and Katie climbed up on my lap and clung so tightly to me that I could not move. Every time I shifted position, she hugged me tighter! I would have loved to have heard what Mrs. Martha said to the woman. When Mrs. Martha came back to the car and we drove off, a shiver went through Katie and suddenly she started crying. I let her cry until she was finished. Then she opened up and started talking about what had happened to her....

She said that she had not been allowed to cry and she didn't know why....

She also talked about a lot of other weird things that we had no reason to doubt.

Finally, she fell restlessly asleep on my lap. My body ached to stretch out but I knew if I laid her down or gave her to someone to hold, she would come up screaming in fright! Finally, we stopped halfway down the valley at a large motel to spend the night. Katie slept for a solid 24 hours. When she awoke the next morning, she declared she was hungry and looked almost as sparkly as she had before the ordeal and ate a big breakfast!

Our final destination was Sacramento and I was happy when the journey was over. The Griffiths, the family who had been taking care of John, now wanted to know if they could also have Katie. I thought she should rest and unwind after what she had been through and said that I would make my decision after I had spoken with Katie.

She wanted to see John again, but she didn't want to leave me and I didn't push her and let her think about it for a couple of days. When I brought up the subject again, she said "yes", she would like to move to John's house, never asking if I would live or visit them.

Letting go of my children was THE HARDEST THING I HAVE EVER DONE in my life!

I had to sign papers agreeing that I would not try to find nor try to see them.

I had an awful time trying to sign that paper!! Mr. Griffith also offered me money to help me as he said; 'Stabilize and get on my feet'. I answered that I was not selling my children to them, I would say 'NO'! But if they took them and raised them in a loving home, I'd agree but NO MONEY! I was offered $5000 pr. child!

I reflected on the adoption as I saw it. Not only was John going to live in a stranger's house, but now, Katie as well- and I would never see them again! I would miss seeing them grow up seeing John get his first tooth and all the other little things that are so memorable from the growing years! I finally signed the papers, leaving me alone with my tears and thoughts in the big city of Sacramento.

Until I could find a job, I lived with relatives of Mrs. Martha, a man, and his sister. They were an absolute delight to be with. She spoke as if she was my age but he was a bit of a 'stuffed shirt'. Then I answered an ad for a 'live-in' housekeeper and got the position.

Mr. and Mrs. T were nice people. Mrs. T was very pretty, a tall and slender lady who immigrated from Europe to the USA after W.W.2. Consequently, she treated her help as servants, and I was no different. I was a servant to her instead of a housekeeper and a human being. She would put on her white glove and check where I had been cleaning, making me paranoid about my work!

After nine months, I couldn't take it anymore. With Mr. T. No problem, he was a nice and quiet man. On my days off, he would wait up and read the paper until I came home safely, then he'd go to bed. One evening I asked him why he did it....

"It's the right thing to do, Randi," he said. "People should take care of their help properly." I thanked him for his care, said 'good night', and went to my room.

Well, I thought 'You obviously don't know what your wife does to me'. When I gave my notice of quitting, he wanted to know why I was leaving so I decided to tell him.

"Mr. T, I would really like to stay but your wife has made it very difficult for me," I began. I could tell he didn't know what she had been up to.

"Any chance of correcting this?" he asked.

"Sorry but no," I admitted.

I immediately got a job with another family whom I learned to love and honor very much! I gathered from their action, that they liked me as well so I guessed- 'It was meant to be this way.'

Mr. and Mrs. B. had three sons; Rodman age 9, Jed age 5, Kurt age 3- and I grew to adore all three!!!

I needed to be out with 'friends' so I joined a folk-dance group to have fun and I began to enjoy life again. I met a girl named Ann who eventually became my best friend and the friendship still goes on to this day! She was going steady with a man who had a friend they wanted me to meet, so they arranged a double date. They didn't want me to feel left out all the time.

"Anyway," Ann said, "You're going to need an escort to the folk-dance festivals and special dances the group will attend."

I had never been on a blind date before. Eventually, I agreed to meet this man. He was tall, with dark blond hair, hazel eyes and a smile that I really fell for was bashful- yet open. I also liked his long, slender hands. But we had one thing in common- we definitely did not like each other at all!! Still, we agreed to be partners for dancing only, nothing else! We discussed what we didn't like about each other and held nothing back! I didn't like that he drank too much and couldn't dance and I thought that he was a 'stick in the mud'! He thought I was too flippant, flighty, and too fat! The latter was true, I had gained some weight, and I developed an ulcer from worry, too much coffee, and too many cigarettes. Mr. B. who was a doctor, had put me on a special diet and recommended that I quit smoking and I started gaining weight when I did quit. When the doctor said it was ok to do, I put myself on a weight loss program upon the doctor's approval and lost all the weight I had gained and more, that made me feel good- I felt desirable again!

Despite our differences, Wylie and I remained partners. One week-end we went with the dance group to a festival in Fresno. While we were waiting for everybody to get ready to dance, Wylie and I started talking about ourselves. He wanted to know more about me. I told him about my rape and what came from that, my beautiful girl Evy and that she lived with my mother in Norway. I wanted to tell him about Katie and John but I let it be at that time. After I finished talking, he became very quiet and looked as if he was deep in thought. A cold hand gripped my body at the thought that I was losing him, not that I cared- but still- I had sort of gotten used to having him around, that's all, I told myself! But soon, our thoughts were interrupted when the group announced that they were ready to leave for the dance. I was so happy to break away from my thoughts.

The whole group stayed in one motel. I stayed in a room with Ann and two other girls. Wylie stayed with some of the men. It was no 'messing around', we all acted like one big family. Ann wanted to know what had happened between Wylie and me, so I told her and also admitted my fear that we were about to part company. She just smiled and said to 'wait and see'.

On the way back up the valley from Fresno toward Sacramento I sat next to Wylie but cleverly avoided talking about anything related to ourselves. He brought me home and left me at my door where we said 'good night' and he drove off.

The following evening the phone rang and it was him, saying he didn't think we should see each other for a while.

"Why?" I asked. There were several moments of silence.

"I told my parents about you, Randi," he began," but my mother doesn't think that I should get mixed up with you, a divorcee and a foreigner to boot!"

That one hurt, my temper flared and I weighed my words very carefully.

"I think you are right; I think we should not see each other at all anymore! Anyone who still has to ask their parents' advice at the age of 26 is not right for me! Anyway, what was all that hoopla about liking European girls better than Americans because they are more level-headed? Did you say that just for my benefit? I'll see you around!" With that, I hung up the phone, walked to my room, and cried. Had I fallen in love with this guy? I wondered. I didn't want to fall in love, because as soon as I had saved enough money for a ticket, I was going home to Norway.

The days dragged by and I worked hard, but I felt like a zombie, every part of me was set on automatic. I thought about the dancing class that was coming up in two days. Would I be able to 'bum' a ride from somebody to get home? I lived so far from the main part of town that I hated to ask anyone. Yet I was too scared to take the bus because I would have to walk half a block past lots of shrubbery, and it just wasn't safe! Wednesday evening Wylie called and apologized for the last conversation we had and said he wanted to see me the next day to talk 'things' out and I agreed. When we met that following afternoon, he told me that he told his mother in so many words to mind her own business. I tried to imagine his mother's reaction. I had met his parents before at a dinner that I was invited to at their house. Wylie's mother was a very thin lady with sharp features and a tongue to match. Although her words were soft, she always said what was on her mind. His father made a big impression on me. He was mild-mannered and gentle with a soft voice and few words to say. Fall turned into winter and for Christmas Wylie gave me 13 red roses. It was the best present and the most romantic present I had ever received, particularly since I had never gotten flowers from a man before. On New Year's Evening, we attended a party together and welcomed in 1964!

Spring came and I had gotten used to having this 'guy' around. Then he 'popped' the question- I said 'YES'! We chose our wedding rings and officially became engaged on my birthday, May 26th. Since my divorce decree was due to be passed on August 5th, we set our wedding date for August 8th, tentatively- with the understanding that we would move the date, if the decree were not finalized by then.

My attorney was happy on my behalf, that I had found happiness at last, but shook his finger at me because I had gotten engaged already.

"Etiquette, you know," he said.

On August 5th, my divorce decree was granted and we could get married on the set date, August 8th. I asked Ann to be my 'maid of honor' and Chris her fiancé, to be my best man. We had found an apartment and I moved in right away, made curtains, and unpacked all my household goods that had been stored for so long. Nobody knew that I had already moved in except us four. If Wylie's mom had known, she would really have been upset, but as far as Wylie and I knew, she never knew.

Wylie and I decided to have a small party the evening before the wedding. We asked Chris and Ann to join us to celebrate. I made German spiced wine from a German recipe.

I also made other delicacies to snack on. I guess we must have had a good time because we all suffered from hangovers the day following. Ann stayed the night with me but neither one of us slept much.

The next morning, I had a hair appointment at 8;30 AM to have my hair done. It felt so good to ride my bicycle in the chill of the morning air. There was almost no traffic that time of the day, so I didn't have to worry. The beautician was 20 minutes late. I just knew that I'd be late to my own wedding! I have never been depicted to be kept waiting for anything, especially now! When she finally arrived, I let her have it. She had no real reason for oversleeping, which didn't sit too well with me at all! When I came back to the apartment, all three were there waiting for me, and we were off to the church in North Sacramento, about a 30-minute drive away.

The ceremony went off without a hitch at 11:00 AM. After we said our vows, we went to a designated restaurant for a champagne brunch, just the four of us and my new father-in-law.

Wylie's mother and my new mother-in-law had decided to fly to South Carolina to visit his sister who were to give birth around the day of our wedding. I found her leaving just too much of a coincidence but went out of my way not to mention her absence. But I could tell Wylie was disappointed that she wasn't there!

We planned to spend our honeymoon driving to Oregon and our designation was Eugene, where we were going to look for property to purchase. When we left Davis, it was 103* in the shade! By the time we came to Redding, the motel clerk said it had reached 117* at noon! I glanced at the thermometer and it read 113* and it was dinner ! But my new husband and I didn't feel the heat- we were too wrapped up in each other!! After we checked in, we showered, changed clothes, and went out to dinner. Neither of us was very hungry, partly from the heat but mostly from the excitement of the day! After he went to sleep, I lay there thinking about how different he was from Einar. He was thoughtful, didn't drink to excess, and didn't smoke at all and he was gentle and soft-spoken. I had not been accustomed to that but I thought I could get used to it now and fell asleep with a smile in my 'wounded' and soon-to-be-healed heart. The next day, neither one of us could recall what we had for dinner the night before, which made us giggle.

When we arrived in Eugene, the weather was cloudy and cool but it felt great after the hot weather we had experienced in CA and the day before.

We bought a map and drove around to familiarize ourselves with the roads around town. The second day, we started looking for property. We stayed in Eugene for one week, but couldn't find any property that would be right for us, and drove back to CA. When we met up with Chris, he asked: "Where did you hide the car before the honeymoon?"

Chapter 9

Wylie smiled his little smile and didn't say a word. Oh, I knew that I had found the companion for my future and the rest of my living days!

I took a job as a housekeeper for a doctor whose husband was a professor at the University of California at Davis. We had been married about 4 months when our friends began to wonder why I wasn't 'showing' yet. They had thought that since we got married so suddenly, I 'had' to be pregnant. We just laughed and assured them that I was not with a child. When we had been married about nine months, I did become pregnant. We had not planned on having any children at all but it seemed that it was meant to be, so we let it happen! I didn't feel well for the first 5 months. But the last 4 were great! I was working well into the 7th month when Wylie became a little worried about me riding my bike back and forth to work. Since it was nearly winter, he was worried about fog and icy roads. When Wylie's mother, (whom I asked if I could call 'mom' and she agreed to it) discovered I had been using my bike for all my mobility around town, she became very upset and demanded that I call her whenever I needed to go somewhere during the day! But that didn't stop me, I still took my daily ride, and for the last three weeks, I walked.

On January 28th, 1966 our baby girl, Heidi Birgitte came to this world. All along in my pregnancy, I knew it would be a girl. The clothes I had bought were pink right down to the diaper pins that had pink heads. My doctor said that it was a boy because of the 'power' he saw in the fetus but I said it was a girl with that power! When she was born, they all got a laugh at all the 'pink' things I had brought to the hospital! Our baby was beautiful, with no red blotches on her skin at all, just pure perfection! Wylie and I had picked out her name long before she was born but just in case it was a boy, we had a boy's name ready as well.

"How about Eric?" he suggested. I said that I liked that name as well. While I was pregnant, we purchased a little Pomeranian puppy and named her Candy. Wylie worked with her through obedience training and we had a lot of fun with her. She became very attached to us, especially Wylie. On the day when our baby came home from the hospital, Wylie carried the baby Heidi, into the house.

Candy was happy to see us and when I greeted her, she licked my hand. Wylie bent down and let her smell the baby, then he petted her. But when he put the baby in her crib, Candy reached over and bit his pants leg in a fit of jealousy, then ran to her bed and refused her evening meal.

We left her alone but assured her that it was all right.

When little Heidi was 4 months old, we moved to Eugene, OR.

The climate there had attracted us and we spoke of it constantly. Along with the climate came the scenery which reminded me of Norway with its many kinds of trees and greenery of all kinds and the lush mountains which surrounded the city. What made me even happier was that it wouldn't be as hot as in Davis. The week before we were to move up there, Wylie flew to Eugene to look for work, which he found in a Volkswagen shop. We loaded up our van with clothing, and a wire cage made for Candy, grabbed Heidi, and headed north! Our furniture was shipped by moving van.

The first year we lived in an apartment, and then we had a house built. It was a nice little 2-bedroom house. For a down payment, we painted the inside ourselves. At the time the kitchen needed paint, Wylie came down with the flu. He stayed home with Heidi while I painted the kitchen and had fun doing it!

The day we moved in, I felt as if I was living in a dream. Imagine-- a new home, a husband who loves me for who I am- myself and my baby girl! The best of all was that my husband never 'went out with the boys'. He had no desire to do so, he said, he had everything he ever wanted right at home. I was swooning with happiness! One day he said that he wanted me to meet the owner of the shop where he worked. A couple of evenings later, we wrapped Heidi up and made the trip to the shop. Sometimes the men would work on their own cars in the evenings and this was such an evening. The owner walked in and Wylie introduced us. I recognized him right away but he kept looking at me, and finally, I asked him if he recognized me. He said he couldn't place me but he did know me from somewhere. I said that I used to work at Piano Roll Inn in Roseburg years before and that he used to call me 'Norsky', then he remembered. We sat and chatted for a while and then we had to leave and tend to Heidi. Wylie and I enjoyed living in this new neighborhood with lots of young people with young kids like ourselves and Heidi enjoyed having many playmates around. We had lived there a couple of years when all of a sudden, I became very homesick! I talked it over with Wylie and he decided to ask his parents about borrowing $1500, -then I could fly home for a visit. They agreed and we developed a plan. I was to stay in Norway with Heidi with my parents through the summer. Wylie's parents would come and stay with him in Eugene. My in-laws had just sold their home, so they put the furniture in storage and came to Eugene. So, the three of them changed their mind and drove to Canada on vacation.

Heidi and I were off to Norway, landing at Kirkenes, where Papa and my brother Sten met us. It was a tearful reunion for all of us. Sten had grown into a young man and Papa had gotten older but it was so good to see them again. During the ride home, Heidi got sick all over my coat and dress but I didn't care as I was much too tired. I made her as comfortable as possible and she fell asleep and slept all the way home.

We arrived home and I walked in, calling her. Mama was asleep on the couch but woke up as I put my arms around her. We cried a bit, but Mama wasn't much for emotions, she straightened her back and got serious. "What are we sitting around here for", she asked, "I've got to fix you all something to eat, you must be hungry".

"Thank you, mama," I answered," I'm not really hungry and Heidi was sick to her stomach all over me on the way here."

She stretched and stood up from the couch and we walked into the kitchen, and she greeted her new granddaughter. But Heidi just wanted to sleep and we let her. Papa, Sten, and Mama had a meal while I had coffee while they ate their noon meal. I was glad that Sten was there because I was mixing English and Norwegian, I was so tired that I hadn't slept in 36 hours. Finally, I had to excuse myself and went and took a nap. Mama woke me two hours later to have supper with them. I still wasn't hungry, even though I hadn't eaten since breakfast on the plane and it was 8 PM.

I ate a little bit and we sat and talked for a while, this time my speech went easier but I soon tired, said 'good night' and went to bed. Heidi slept until morning without waking up.

It was fun to visit my village again. Since it's such a small place, with only 7-800 inhabitants, everyone knows everyone else's business, what they eat at mealtime, and so on!

There are a few people I'd rather not have spoken with but I decided to 'bury the ax'! People were thinking that I had become wealthy since I could come home and stay so long. Others guessed that I had separated from my husband.

During our visit, Sten entered the hospital for a very serious operation. He had a polyp growing in one of his sinus canals, with a complication. The polyp had wrapped itself around a major blood vessel that fed the left side of his body and in particular, his face. The surgeons had to open his chest to tie off the vein in order to remove the polyp, he spent 1 month in the hospital. While this was going on, I felt more and more alienated from Mama and Papa. They would stop talking when I entered the room. I realized what a difficult time they were having with Sten's hospital stay and tried to talk about it, but neither one would open up. I called the hospital and spoke with the doctor who said he had orders from the parents of silence, even to Sten's sister! I let it go and rode it out! He came home 3 days before I left for the USA again. One afternoon Sten and I were sitting in the kitchen with a coffee cup, and I asked if we could open up and talk freely. He agreed but never had much to say. I would catch him looking at me with a puzzled look as if he wanted to speak with his big sister but didn't know how to start and he never did start a conversation.

Two months after my arrival, Evy finished school for the year and I looked forward to getting to know her better. We had been apart for so many years. She attended school in an adjacent town, a 3-hour bus ride from our village. During the school year, she would come home on Saturday and be with her friends for most of the time, then leave with the bus on Sunday afternoon, which didn't leave much time for Heidi and me. So, when school was out for the year, we had lots more time for the three of us to spend together. The weeks rolled by so fast and I had to insist upon Heidi speaking English or she would have forgotten how-to all together. As it was, she would answer my English in Norwegian!

Mama really enjoyed Heidi and Heidi her as well. Soon it was time to go back to Eugene, where I had mixed feelings. I wanted to see Wylie again, but I didn't want to leave my family, especially Evy, who was a beautiful 14-year-old young lady, but I knew I had to go. The same with Heidi, she didn't want to go either. She had learned to love the family and had the whole village' in her pocket'! She would walk into a store and they handed her candy any time. The store owners thought her accent was so cute and rewarded her for learning to speak Norwegian as fast as she did! It was a tearful 'goodbye' and Mama stayed home while Evy, Sten, and Papa drove us to the airport and saw us off. The flight back to Eugene seemed twice as long and exhausting as the trip to Norway. I knew it was because we were going back to the everyday grind of life. All Heidi would talk about was all the friends and family she left behind in Norway! We arrived in Eugene late in the afternoon and were so tired that we fell into bed. The following day Heidi got up early as she had been accustomed to doing in Norway. There she would get up and have her breakfast with Mama and sit and talk with her. She did the very same thing in Eugene then when I awoke, I found an extremely upset mother-in-law. Heidi couldn't speak English at all, she barely understood! I tried to explain the situation, how difficult it had been to keep up her English since she played with Norwegian children, but Mom couldn't or wouldn't understand! She blamed it all on me, said it was my fault, and that I should have done a better job in keeping her English up!

I kept quiet and let her carry on, it was no use to try to reason with her! I just couldn't figure out where all this resentment toward me came from. What had I done that was so bad? Since Wylie never talked back to his mom or tried to stick up for me, I felt so alone when she started in on me! Although Wylie seemed to enjoy Heidi and her speech, they communicated just fine and had fun while they did!! Heidi's friends on our street enjoyed listening to her as well. They would ask her a question and she would answer in Half Norwegian, half English, and the others thought it was great fun listening. Mom and Dad drove back to CA and I slipped into my wifely- role again. My little family was once again complete! After I got settled, I started feeling as if something was missing from my life, so I began searching.

One day I read an advertisement. It was an ad about a book on the 'compiled sixth and seventh books of Moses, from the Bible. I ordered the book, but little did I know that the material I was about to read was about black Magic and Witchcraft exclusively! Along with the book came several pamphlets of incantations and spells of all kinds to be performed. I started reading and really thought that I had found what I had been looking for! I started practicing spells and the incantations and began to feel 'alive'! After a while, I began to have trouble sleeping at night.

I would wander around the house in the dark, and when the moon was full, I could not sleep until dawn. I would go to bed when Wylie did, but I would wake up when I heard someone call my name and be wide awake the rest of the night! I started hearing voices at all hours of day and night and became worried that something was seriously wrong with me. I telephoned several pastors around town explaining my problem, but everyone I spoke with politely refused to listen to me! One dared to insinuate that I had a medical problem, which upset me greatly! I suggested that maybe he wasn't fit to say The Lord's name and the name of the church and promptly hung up on him. I decided to give up on churches! I had a feeling that I was supposed to solve this problem all by myself and decided to tackle the Bible first!

When I began with 'the black arts', I learned that one is not supposed to touch the Bible at any time. Since I felt I was not ready to become a witch, I picked up the Good Book. It felt so hot to the touch that I almost dropped it! Noice invaded my ears and I felt so dizzy that I could hardly stand it. Automatically, I started leafing through the chapters- my fingers stopped by a verse that translated to me in a special way. I took it to say that if I didn't change my way of thinking and my actions as of this day, my life would be damned for eternity!

Suddenly, I found myself sitting on the floor in a corner of our living room, with the Bible in my hands without knowing how I got there. Wylie walked in the door from his work and saw me and promptly demanded to know what had happened! I saw his lips move but I heard no sounds. I tried to speak, but my tongue would not function. Wylie took my shoulders and shook hard as he demanded an answer. When none came, he slapped me across the face in desperation then held me close, rocking me back and forth assuring me all would be alright. I finally got my voice back and started sobbing. After my crying died down, I could finally tell him what had been going on during those past four months! The Bible suddenly dropped out from my hands and I bent over to pick it up and discovered it was not hot anymore to the touch! I felt so happy that I started crying again. At that time, I experienced a feeling of lightness as if I were floating above the floor somewhere. I tried to explain the feeling to him, but I didn't know if he could understand. The weeks passed and I poured through the Bible, trying to find the passage that had saved me. Instead, I found one that suggested not to dwell on the past but look to the future, so I did! After this horrific experience, I began to notice something else. I would think of something and moments later, Wylie would express similar words! If I thought of something that needed to be done, he would do it and say he just thought of it! One day while I was standing and ironing, I had a sudden attack of extreme fear. I knew someone close to me was in mortal trouble and I started crying! I called Wylie at work but he was fine. I then sat down and wrote Mama, demanding an immediate reply and I did. I received her reply two weeks later, where she said that Sten had to have a second sinus surgery. While he was on the operating table, something went wrong and he died for however many seconds but the doctors managed to revive him! Two months later, another strange thing happened one day as I felt especially tired and decided to take a nap along with Heidi after we had our lunch. I heard a knock on the door, and the front door opened and closed. I walked out to the living room and there stood my mother. We embraced, talked, and laughed and she teased me about sleeping during the day. I awoke. It had been a dream. I noted the time and promptly wrote to Mama, describing what she wore and how she looked. I couldn't believe the letter I got back from her. At that prescribed time she was on board a plane bound for the hospital in Oslo for a surgical procedure, wearing the same clothes as in my dream. At the time I 'saw' her, her thoughts had gone to me and my family as she wondered how we were doing.

Soon after this happened, I began daydreaming about Norway, thinking about how nice it would be to live there again. I realized how much I had missed my country, with its wild mountains, green meadows, tall trees, and colorful houses. I longed to breathe fresh sea air again!

One day I mentioned my daydream to Wylie. He thought about the prospect of moving to Norway for a while, then he suggested we send for tourist information on a little town called Hamar, located in the southeastern part of the country. When we received the brochures, we liked what we read. Wylie thought it would be nice to move there. However, the immigration law stipulated that in order to enter Norway, one first had to have a guaranteed job there. I wrote Papa and said what we were about to do. We received a letter back stating that there was a job waiting for Wylie when he arrived! Immigration sent a couple of papers for us to sign. Since I was still a citizen of Norway and would be returning, I had no problems. It also went smoothly for Wylie and Heidi. We sent our documents on our way, updated our passports, and then held a huge garage sale to get rid of all our household items. We were lucky to sell them all. The only things we had left were dishes, pots and pans, linen, and our own clothes. The worst part of our preparation was when Wylie had to tell his parents about our move.

He waited until they came to visit us. We all drove to Cottage Grove to ride a special train called "THE GOOSE". It was an old steam-driven train that took tourists into the mountains. Heidi and I sat toward the front so that Wylie could speak with his parents privately. His dad gave us his blessings but his mother was quite another matter. She told Wylie to give me a 'one-way' ticket and let me go home!! I knew she would be hurt at the thought of her only son moving so far away, but lashing out at me like that really hurt! Wylie was also very surprised at her outburst and wasn't going to tell me but he finally did.

I sat there with thoughts whirling through my head. How could she say that? Did she hate me that much? Although I knew that she had never liked me very much. Despite how she had implored Wylie to marry an American girl who was a virgin, he did neither and to top it off, I was divorced! Why was she lashing out at me now?

But I still couldn't hate her, it wasn't within my heart to do so, especially since she had given birth to my husband! But what did I feel toward her? I didn't know but I promised myself that I would forgive her before they went back to CA.

The day before they left, Mom suggested they should take Heidi with them back to CA. That way we could concentrate on packing and all the other details of our move. As she spoke, she looked at me with eyes mild as a sunny spring morning. They definitely had the words 'I'm sorry' in them, even though Mom would never utter those words out loud. In all the years I knew her, I cannot remember her ever saying that. Instead, she would show how sorry she was by doing things for me, like taking Heidi with them now. Our house sold right away and we shipped our household goods ahead to Norway. Then we rented a car and drove to CA to pick up Heidi. She was happy to see us. We stayed a couple of days to visit friends to say 'good-bye' before driving back to Eugene. On the last evening before we left and after Heidi had gone to bed, the four of us sat and talked about things that concerned the family. Our future plans and Norway were not mentioned, and although Wylie and I exchanged glances, we didn't bring up the subject. The following morning, we had breakfast early, and then we readied ourselves for the long drive back to Oregon. We all hugged each other and I noticed that mom's eyes were as moist as mine were. Who was she sorry to see go? I wondered. Was it Wylie or Heidi or both? It was most certainly not me.

We left Eugene for Norway in April 1972, our destination was Hamar, a picturesque little town with a population of 28000. The town is nestled against the mountains. Norway's largest lake, the Mjosa, lies at Hamar's feet. We liked the atmosphere right away. When we first arrived, we had to stay at a hotel for a week while Wylie looked for a job there. My father had promised work but he and the rest of my family, live up north above the 45* border and I knew Wylie would not acclimate for a long time, maybe years. But Hamar is situated on what Norwegians call the 'banana belt' which means that it's a lot warmer and fruit grows there. Wylie discovered that General Motors had an auto shop there and was owned by a person who had lived in New York for many years and was married to a woman from Seattle, WA.

Wylie applied for a job and got it right away, as the shop needed a mechanic who was familiar with re-building and alignment of car front ends. They were very pleased to get someone that knew what to do, and so they didn't have to send them to school to learn how-to! Until we could find a place to live, Mr. Flaatrud Wylie's boss, offered to lend their summer cabin for us to live in until we could find a place. (In Norway, it's extremely difficult to find housing)We had to sign our name on a list and we checked on our no and how far down on the list we were and saw we were 17995 and it would be 3 to 5 years before our name came up! But for a couple of thousand dollars (under the table,) we would have it in about a week. This cabin stood a 20 minute-bus ride from town and was a 2-story house with a panoramic view for the living room's bay windows of Hamar. It was pointed out to us that we would be able to see 5 counties. Each county has a church spire, and we counted, and sure enough- it was 5 spires clearly visible. We accepted the housing offer gladly; anything was better than living in an expensive hotel! We decided not to put our name on the list and to take our chances. "The cabin" as Flaatrud called it, lay nestled against a small hill on a plateau overlooking the town. It had 2 small bedrooms upstairs. Downstairs were the front hall, kitchen, dining room, and a sunken living room with a huge fireplace. The place was totally furnished, and decorated in 'old world' with colors of old red and blue with natural wood tones. The kitchen was painted in white and light blue. There were no hot water tanks, the water had to be heated on the range! We had electricity but no TV. No toilet either- the outhouse lay 25 ft. from the main house. It was no fun on chilly evenings before bed to use the 'Biffy' to satisfy bodily functions!

About 1 ft. away from the outhouse ran a fence with a pasture on the other side, where horses were kept. When it was time to go to bed, always regular as clockwork, the horses would start their exercising hour. Sitting in the outhouse and having the horses run by, was extremely eerie! Since the fence was only ten ft. past the outhouse, the horses would stop right by the outhouse and neigh as they played their 'game' with each other, all 5 of them! At twilight, the three of us would sit and look out the window and we'd see wild rabbits and foxes dart across the yard.

Although the scenery was beautiful, the cabin didn't have much in the way of conveniences. We had to carry water from a well across the road. Since we had electricity, we warmed it in a large pan on the range. I truly learned how to conserve water! About a 15-minute walk from the cabin stood a small grocery store, where the bus makes the 'turn-around.' I used to walk to the store every day with Heidi, mainly for exercise. The store owners were nice people but extremely reserved. I found this to be true with most people around Hamar or maybe most of the population of the country as a whole. They are reserved until they get to know you, then you have their unconditional friendship!

Doing laundry was quite a chore. First, I'd carry water (twice the amount) from the well. To half the amount, I'd add detergent then warm it on the range overnight and in the morning, I'd pour it into the large tub that doubles as a bath tub, rub the clothes on a knuckle board, wring them, and carry them across the road to the well where I would rinse them 6-7 times. Wring out well then hang on the line to dry! Whew!!! Bathing was also quite an event! I would also carry double the amount of water and heat it on the range before pouring it into the large tub and taking our bath. Heidi enjoyed the bath greatly! I did ALL the heavy work around the house because I couldn't or wouldn't ask Wylie. He was really working hard. He had to leave early to catch the 6:10 AM bus, in order to be at work at 7 AM. He was always tired when he came home. Not only from working but mentally worn out from trying so hard to learn Norwegian. I didn't mind any of the hard work, because I loved being 'home' in Norway again and hearing my own language being spoken and being able to speak it myself once again! There were times when I would make myself a cup of coffee, sit down in the living room, and lose myself in the beautiful view. Those were the times when I would find tears rolling down my face from the love of the scenery of my homeland and realize how much I've missed.

Chapter 10

Wylie seemed to enjoy what he was doing but Heidi had a problem. She wanted to play with the neighborhood children, but the language barrier prevented that, so she stayed home most of the time. Sometimes, during the day she would come in crying from anger and sadness because the neighbors' children rejected her. I would try to console her, but I never intervened. I felt and also suggested to her that she should pick up the words and use them, that's the way to learn to speak.

We had been living in the cabin for 2 months. When Wylie heard that one of the workers at his shop was planning to move from an apartment that stood one block from the shop. The apartment building also belonged to the Flaatrud family. We applied for the apt. and got it, and moved in 3 weeks later! This building was a two-story complex with 1,2-, and 3-bedroom apartments inside. There was also a large attic made into a smaller apt. The building was 120 years old with rooms with 10 ft. ceilings and 6ft windows. We got 2 bedrooms, a nice kitchen and best of all, a bathroom with a toilet!

The living room had a built-in oil heater. I enjoyed going shopping for the furniture we needed. Before we left the cabin, we had purchased a car, an OPEL. While Wylie was working, I would visit furniture stores, then when he came home at 3:30, we would drive to the stores so he could see what I had chosen.

Heidi was very excited about the prospect of brand-new furniture! It felt good to choose the furniture largely on my own, and then have enough money to pay cash for the whole lot! Since we paid cash, the delivery was free of charge. In one swoop, we furnished the whole apartment except the kitchen range, which came with the apartment. Getting my work done at the apt. was so much easier than the cabin, at least I didn't have to carry water or use the outhouse. I did have to use the basement, however. There was a wood stove with a huge kettle. I would load the kettle with water, add detergent and clothes, light a fire under the kettle, and let the clothing soak until the next morning, when I would stoke the fire again and when the clothes were warmed thoroughly. wash them and rinse well and wring them well also. Then carry them to the loft where they will be hung to dry. In the winter, doing laundry was not fun, because it was cold and tiring, but deep down I felt it was fun as well, too.

A couple of streets from the apartment was a huge soccer field that doubled as a skating rink in the winter. The city would flood the field with water. After it froze, men and women in Olympic Training would come to practice there. We purchased Skates for both Heidi and Wylie. She would come home with exciting tales about the Russian and American stars she had met that day. Once she came home giggling. She had fallen and slid into an American man who helped her up.

"He was so nice and handsome"! She said and giggled.

Wylie would skate but he had to re-learn because he was used to figure skates but now, he was using speed skates!

We settled in town and enjoyed every moment of it. Every day Heidi became more accustomed to the language. Two apt.'s down from us lived a girl named Karin. The two of them became best friends and to our surprise, Heidi picked up the dialect of Hamar very quickly! Wylie picked up the language very quickly as well. He would analyze each sentence to understand the meaning of each word and then proceed slowly until he understood. I was pleased when he started building sentences on his own. One thing that slowed him down was the mountain dialect that the Hamar population used. When folks spoke with him, they would have to speak slowly and clearly so he could understand. After a while, he could converse with most of them.

One day he came home from work extremely upset. A customer had come to the shop to have his car repaired and when he found out Wylie was an American, he started saying all kinds of unkind words. The owner of the shop was called. He asked the man to leave and not come back unless he had an apology ready, the man just snorted, got into his car, and left! A couple of weeks later, my father phoned and asked if Wylie was interested in starting an auto shop in my home village. Papa was willing to pay for the move and all but we knew he would not be able to handle the harsh climate there. In the winter, the climate falls below zero every day, and there are lots of snowstorms. The springs and falls are also cool and the summers are filled with lots of mosquitoes. Around this time, we started entertaining the notion of going back to the USA. When he got his 4-week vacation during the summer of 1973, we decided to drive up to my hometown before leaving Norway for good.

At first, we had planned to drive the length of Norway. But we found out from some who had done it that it would take a week of driving and waiting for car ferries and decided to drive through Sweden and Finland to reach Northern Norway. The drive was beautiful- there was so much to see. In Sweden, we met up with an elk and her twin calves who were walking along the highway. Finland was even more picturesque, with gently rolling hills and green meadows dotted with houses. We were amazed at how clean the towns were. Then we came to a stretch in the road that led us along the edge of Finland's largest lake, Inari. The water seemed to go on forever and was lovely to see. Since we were above the Polar circle, we experienced the Midnight sun, which made it hard to sleep when we stayed at a youth hostel in Rovaniemi. Part of the road alongside the lake was under construction. We had to drive 3 hours on a roadbed of large, crushed rocks. After all that bouncing around, we were sore all over. When we finally came to a paved road, we joined several other cars that had stopped along the road to rest before continuing. After spending a day and a half on the road, we reached my hometown at 6;30 PM and began a 4-week visit! Mama and Papa fell in love with Wylie and couldn't believe how much Heidi had grown since they saw her last, in 1970. I was so proud of my husband and daughter. Wylie met Evy, who was now 16 years old. Being a person of few words, Wylie said very little, and Evy even less. She had grown into a lovely girl with a sparkling smile, she was slim, almost skinny! I felt as if a bond was being formed between Evy and my little family. I couldn't explain as to why I felt like this, I just did! Heidi was beside herself with happiness over her big sister that she hadn't seen in three long years but Evy was very reserved toward Heidi. Wylie thought my brother Sten was very interesting and learned a lot from him, Wylie said. Papa and Wylie hit it off right away. They were both soft-spoken men and according to Sten, had several interesting conversations. Mama shared Papa's feelings for Wylie and thought he could do no wrong, which made me happy and content. The four weeks flew by, and then it was time to say 'goodbye'. We knew it would be a long time before we saw each other again. A couple of months later Evy came down to Hamar and moved in with us. At first, I was very happy that she had come to me, but then the situation grew tense. She didn't want us to act like 'parents'. She would stay out very late, then a few hours later have to get up and go to work. Being as tired as she was all the time she was constantly in a bad mood and I didn't know where the fault lay. Wylie and I had never handled a teenager, an unruly one at that and she didn't know how to handle young parents since she was used to my parents, eventually, she moved out.

January 1974, we decided to move back to the USA that year and set our departure date for June. Then I found out that I had lost my resident visa. I wrote to the Immigration office and they sent back a thirty-page questionnaire to fill out.

Then I found out that I had lost my resident visa through an oversight— Although no one had told me that I was supposed to have gone back to the USA after one year to keep up my residency. Since we had been gone for two years, I had to re-apply!

After I sent off the papers, I received a letter informing me that I couldn't leave at the chosen time because the quota to the USA had been filled! I could leave at a later date, but didn't state how much later! The questionnaire also had a discrepancy that needed to be discussed. I called the Embassy in Oslo and made an appointment for the following week. Wylie and I took the train to Oslo, while Heidi stayed with a friend. Luckily, we were able to straighten the whole mess out. It seemed that Immigration had cross-filed the papers….

They thought I was still married to my first husband Einar and therefore I had no reason to leave Norway. They said that they understood but there was another problem, much bigger. It seemed that Einar for a time, was involved with the Communist movement in some way and so I had some hard questions to answer. This was new news to me, and said I had not heard of that before but I was not believed at all! The result was that they sent me another questionnaire, with some 200 questions to be answered in record time!

Our first papers came and we were allowed to leave The Country but the papers answering my questions were still out!

The waiting period was awful in every way but finally- three weeks later- they arrived! I saw myself being left behind, having to wait a year or more to join my husband and child. Wylie confessed later that he had also worried about that.

June came and it was time to move. We had a moving sale and sold it all, in one weekend! The night before we left, we stayed at a friend's house. The following day we took the train to Oslo on the first 'leg' of our journey back to Eugene.

Then the plane to Copenhagen, Denmark. Our plane was late taking off from Denmark because of a mechanical problem. When we arrived in Seattle, all our corresponding flights had left. The airline made arrangements for all 75 passengers who had missed their flights. We received hotel rooms, dinner, and breakfast, all free of charge!

Wylie, Heidi, and I grabbed a bite to eat at the hotel restaurant. Heidi announced that she'd like a hamburger with fries, something she hadn't tasted in 2 ½ years! She took one bite and declared; "It's not as good as the Norwegian hot dog!"

Wylie and I had a good laugh. We were too tired to eat, but had a small bite, then we went to bed. When we arrived in Eugene the following day, we were met at the airport by a friend of ours, Darcy. We stayed with her and her family until we found a place of our own. A week later, we found an apartment, and Wylie was lucky enough to find a job as a mechanic at the local transit district shop. In September, Heidi started school. The school system, being true to their name, put her in first grade. I 'hit the ceiling' and went to the school to speak with the principal and her teacher.

"She's already had first grade in Norway," I explained," and she will turn 9 in January."

The teacher tested her and concluded that the child indeed knew her basic three R's and more and by rights academically should be in second grade.

"But I'm bound by the system here," the principal insisted. "Since your daughter has not had first grade in this country, she cannot move up to second grade."

What I found out later was that they didn't know HOW TO handle bilingual kids. They believed that Heidi's English was not clear enough and would sometimes blurt out Norwegian when she got excited!

Wylie and I didn't know what to do. Nobody seemed to care enough to give us any advice as to where to turn in our plight, so we let her stay in first grade, a decision we later came to regret dearly.

After a while, Wylie and I both grew tired of living in an apartment and decided to buy a house. We found a 'just built' three-bedroom house not too far from where we were living and much closer to Heidi's school. This made her happy because she didn't like to ride the school bus! Now she could walk, just like she did in Norway. Sometimes we would compare the two and have a good laugh.

Wylie worked the graveyard shift so he always slept during the day.

For a while I stayed home and got bored also, I found myself thinking too much of my loved ones in Norway, especially Evy. I made a decision to take a part-time job. But what could I do with just a high school diploma? Then it hit me— Why not do house cleaning for people? I started scanning want ads and making phone calls, and before I knew it, I had more jobs than I could handle! The good thing was – that I was always home by the time Heidi came home from school. We would sit and enjoy our little talks of 'events' of the day, I with my coffee and Heidi with her snack. After sharing, Heidi did her homework if she had any to do, was free for the rest of the day, and went to find her friends until dinner.

Between 5;00 and 5;30 Wylie would wake up and have supper with us, spend a couple of hours with Heidi before she went to bed. It wasn't much of a life for us as a family, those 8 years he worked the graveyard shift but at least it was a job- and Heidi and I adapted as best we could.

We virtually had no social life because Wylie always felt tired. If we went to a movie, inevitably he would fall asleep.

Time went by and before we knew it, we had lived in our house one whole year.

Wylie was becoming concerned about the neighborhood. Our street had become increasingly busy and crowded with cars, which made it very dangerous for Heidi to cross alone. We started looking for another place to live.

We heard of a new area in another part of town where new houses were being built and we took a look. It was in a different school district from the current one she was in but the area was very nice. We went to talk with the builder about having a house built from preliminary drawings Wylie had drawn, combining German and Norwegian house plans and showed them to the architect, Mr. Smith, who was very enthusiastic. "I'm going to have fun with this plan," he said. It's fun to have something out of the ordinary, to work with because it gets so tedious to always work with tract house plans all the time!"

Wylie's plans needed only a few changes to meet the building code.

We watched our house being built from the first stick of wood hammered in because we drove to the lot every week-end to watch the progress.

On Dec.1977, we moved into our new story-and-a-half European-style home!

The move took three days, but there were a couple of reasons for that! The first reason was freezing rain that made the roads into 'skating rinks' and made it almost impossible for us to back into our new and slightly slanted driveway with our small trailer and car with a heavy load. Reason number two was that I got the flu at Christmas, so for most of the move, it was up to Wylie and Heidi. That little girl worked really hard and really showed what she was made of. She worked side by side with her father carrying smaller items while he lifted the bigger items and she did not complain at all of being tired and I didn't forget her work so when we were moved in and all was settled, I asked her what she wanted for stepping in and helping like she did- money or go to the mall to buy something she might want and she opted for the latter. She and I took a mother-daughter time at the mall and she chose what she wanted.

After the final moving day, I began to feel a little better, had more energy, and was able to lend a hand, but Heidi watched me like a hawk. When she thought I had worked long enough, she ordered me to sit down and rest. But I couldn't rest because every time I sat down, I noticed all the boxes everywhere and all the items that needed to be put away. When they went to the old house to pick up more goods, I would work as fast as possible to put as much as I could away before they came back, even so, it was many days before it was all arranged just right.

Tabitha, our cat came with the final load and took up residence in one of the kitchen cabinets, where she stayed 3 days. Only came out to use her bathroom, 'the potty box'. After we finished the move with the last load, we went out for hamburgers for dinner so I didn't have to cook! We loved our new home!

From the first day, it somehow felt as if all three of us would stay there for a long time, an odd feeling! We had a nice backyard for a garden and flowers with all kinds of landscape possibilities!

As time passed by, I wasn't satisfied with my personal progress. After Heidi was born, I had gained a lot of weight gradually, and had by then, gotten used to carrying it around. I wanted to get rid of it in the worst way and joined Weight Watchers and managed to lose 17 lbs. But with that program, I was thinking of food 24 hours a day, so I quit and unfortunately gained 17 lbs plus 28 more back!

One day, out of curiosity, I attended a meeting of Overeaters Anonymous, which had just come to our town. I became more and more interested in their philosophy and soon discovered that I was not the only 'closet eater' in Eugene. I met people I could identify with and I came to realize that I didn't have to look at myself from the shoulders and up. Now I could Look at the whole 'me' in love instead of disgust and say to that person in the mirror "I LOVE YOU" and mean it!

That was a whole new world and concept to me!! This was a difficult period in my life with some new and hard lessons to learn as I had to face up to my eating problem. Some of my friends could not understand what it was like to binge a couple of weeks at a time. During these times, I would cook up all that fattening food that I grew up with and then I would eat and eat. Sometimes, I ate so much that I would become physically ill and have to vomit!

My binges would not happen when I was happy but as soon as a problem came along, I would start the mad cycle again. It's a problem I will have to live with for the rest of my natural life!

Heidi did quite well in Elementary School and was well-liked in Junior High but when she started in High School, things began to change.

When most young people start High school, they try to see how fast they can turn their parents' hair grey, and again- Heidi was no exception to the rule!

Her freshman year went fine, but a crisis occurred during her second year. Another female student, who had just moved to the area from another state, decided to start calling Heidi 'trash' because Heidi carried a few extra pounds on her frame. This student gathered the few friends she could one evening and lay in wait for her when came outside from having attended a youth group at a church and threatened to beat her up. Luckily, a neighbor happened by and offered her a ride home. That night she came close to hysteria. She cried herself to sleep while I sat by her bed.

Halfway through the school year, I got a call from her home-based class teacher. "Heidi has been skipping a lot of her classes," he told me. "She's seemed to have lost the 'spark' she used to have when she worked."

As he related this, I began to reflect on how moody and restless she had become lately. That evening, I decided to have a talk with her. Throughout her life, I had tucked her into bed and kissed her 'good night' every night. Lately, however, she resisted this tradition and would close the bedroom door with a 'don't bother me' message in her eyes. I would go to bed asking my 'Higher Power' for guidance.

"I'd like to speak with you, Heidi," I asked when she came home that evening. "So, what do you say, let's have a 'rap session?'"

Then I told her about the meeting with her teacher.

"Please level with me," I pleaded.

At first, she became very aggressive and angry. She blamed her father and myself for bringing her up as an only child. Then she blamed the teachers for not being able to teach her anything!

At this point, I really started listening, for I felt instinctively that there was a clue in there somewhere!

"When did you first start experiencing these thoughts?" I asked carefully.

She stared at the floor before she answered, "A couple of months ago."

I felt so bad for her and ached to put my arms around her and tried but she pushed me away. I could almost feel how deeply she hurt inside. It must be something more to this, I thought and it has to come out sooner than later. She was quiet for a while so I made my move and sat down next to her, put my arm around her, and gave her a tiny squeeze. "Honey, would you like to tell me the whole story now?" I asked gently.

She whirled around suddenly and stared at me with hard black eyes. When she was angry her brown eyes would change color to black. For an instant, I thought she was going to slap me, but tears welled up in her eyes as she nodded and straightened herself on the couch. I made a move to sit opposite of her but she grabbed my hand and held on.

Once she started talking, the words came as if you opened a dam. She stopped briefly to draw a breath and with renewed strength, went on and on. First, she talked about the social pressures between upper- and middle-class students. Then she told me about the more serious pressures of drugs.

"I've been smoking pot," she admitted, "but I got sick, I don't like not being in control of my body!"

"When it comes to drugs and weapons on the school grounds, the teachers and the administrators usually look the other way," she continued, "They never make any surprise attacks on kids who are smoking on the school grounds."

She told me that she had learned not to 'tattle' on any of her classmates about their drug habits or exchanges because her life had been threatened several times.

Then she abruptly changed the 'theme' to her academic performance.

"I skip classes because I'm bored," she began." I've tried to talk to the teachers about it, especially my home base teacher and I've even talked to my counselor.

But nobody wants to listen and say that 'it's all in my head' and that I'm lazy!" At this point, she stopped and took a deep breath asking if she could have a cup of hot chocolate. We both went to the kitchen, where I made her a cup from scratch. When it was ready I set it in front of her, but she just sat and stared. Finally, I put my arms around her and held her tightly. Tears came for both of us and we just stood there, held on, and cried. The rivers of tears finally stopped and we looked at each other. "I love you; you know that, right?" I spoke.

"I know mama, but I can't say that in return just yet."

It was painful to hear her say that but I knew someday she would return those words. She sipped her cocoa and I, my coffee.

I asked her, "Do you have a solution to your problems?"

She looked at me as if I had jerked her out of deep thoughts and her hazel eyes opened wide as she said:" As a matter of fact I do", with power behind each word.

"Let's hear it"!

"Don't get upset, mama but I have been doing a bit of research lately. I have come to the conclusion that the best thing I can do is to change schools! I want to leave high school and finish at community college. That way I can finish high school and start college all on one campus!"

At that moment, I felt immensely proud of our girl but my pride was tinged with sadness, a sadness at the thought of my little girl growing up.

"Are you sure about this now, that this is what you want to do?" I asked.

"I am," She answered firmly. Then she yawned and said, "It's bedtime now."

I glanced at the clock and discovered that we had been talking for 4 hours and followed her up the stairs to her bedroom where I tucked her in and kissed her 'good night'.

Then I went to my bedroom and thanked my 'higher power' for hearing my prayers and sending my girl back to me.

Wylie had changed working hours and was now on 'swing shift' and wasn't home. I felt no need to bother him with this, especially since he confided that he didn't know how to handle teenagers anyway.

"You seem to be able to handle them with more ease and patience than I ever could," he once said.

But with this latest, I really needed his input because it was too big for me to handle alone. The day after I spoke with Heidi, I spoke with him and together we decided to make an appointment with the counselor at the high school. Heidi was paged when we arrived for our meeting and the three of us spoke with him. Then the counselor walked us all to see the principal and his assistant principal. They asked her many questions and she fired questions back at them. The room was quiet while notations were made, and then the principal smiled and said to Heidi:" I suggest you set a date for the hearing before the next board meeting!"

On the morning of the hearing Wylie, Heidi, and I waited outside the boardroom. "I'm nervous," Heidi admitted. "As am I, honey!" I admitted. To my surprise, Wylie put his arm around her for comfort!

"You will do just fine!" he assured her.

Then the board secretary opened the hearing.

"Don't be nervous, Heidi," the principal said, "you are among friends here!"

Heidi smiled a nervous smile and thanked him.

"Why have you decided to change schools?" the secretary opened the hearing.

Heidi began reading a statement she had prepared. As she read, my mouth fell open in surprise! I had never heard such well-spoken English come from her mouth before!

As she stated her facts and reasons, there were no such statements as "I guess" "I hope" or "I wish", just facts as she saw them. Some of her statements were very much to the point, I noticed proudly. When she was done, there were a few polite closing remarks before the hearing adjourned. One week later, Heidi received a letter telling her to finish her schooling at college and finally, we all could relax. She entered college and made top grades all the way through. She especially enjoyed meeting young people her own age and was also glad that she wasn't held back in her favorite subjects any longer. Now she could really put her heart and soul into her work.

She also had a lot of support from her teachers there. Instead of holding her back, they helped to further her progress. This may be a problem in some schools, and some students find a subject that holds special interest to them. But instead of furthering their progress, they are held back so the rest of the class can catch up. As a result, the students grow tired and bored like Heidi did.

I was happy that Heidi had finally settled in school for as fall turned into winter I found I had something else to worry about! I began to feel pain and weakness in my lower back and down my left leg. I decided to increase my exercises at the spa and also started a weight loss program, but my efforts were to no avail, the pains became worse.

Our family doctor sent me to a neurologist who admitted me to the hospital where I underwent surgery- my first laminectomy.

Being in the hospital was not a new experience for me as I was there the year prior for another surgery. Even though I was hurting, it was nice to be catered to for my every whim. My surgery went great and I was released 3 days later. I had an allergic reaction to my meds and cracked the other side of the disk and on Dec. 27, I was readmitted to the hospital. This time I was in a wheelchair as my legs wouldn't function. Since my doctor would be out of town until after New Year, I was put in traction until he came back. On Jan. 3 he operated again! This time when I was released, I was in a wheelchair. It was a scary time for me, in particular the first two therapy sessions. The therapist asked me to lift my bottom off the table to tilt my pelvis. In my mind, I saw myself doing it, but in reality, nothing happened.

The therapist explained my dilemma in a way I could understand.

"When you have two surgeries this close together, the body has to shut down some functions in order to concentrate on healing," she said. "It will come back- but you are going to have to work at it through exercise!"

I began to exercise several times during the day. At first, it was the most difficult thing I had ever done.

Meanwhile, Heidi was extremely worried.

"Will you ever walk again, or will you have to use the wheelchair for the rest of your life?" she finally asked.

Her concern brought tears to my eyes and there were hugs all around!

"Not if I have anything to say about it!" I replied.

After two weeks of intense therapy at the hospital, I was transferred to therapy at my spa. Since I already was a member, I could use the whirlpool and other facilities there.

Since Wylie worked for the transit district, I rode free on the buses on special minibuses equipped for wheelchairs and I used the buses to get to the spa. The driver would help me to my front door, unlock the door for me, and make sure I made it in the door, then he would leave!

Little things that most of us take for granted, became hard work for me the first few months. I felt a lot of despair and hopelessness when my body refused to follow my commands and I spent a lot of my time in meditation.

I think this was the time of my life when I started feeling like a flower opening to receive the sunlight- It's the only way to describe this feeling of insight that I now was experiencing....

I began to 'see' a certain person or a 'thing' only to hear from that person or find the 'thing' I saw in my mind!

When St. Helen blew in May 1980, I 'felt' it! That morning when I awoke, I could not move my right arm! Thinking that I'd had a stroke and trying to find the words to give my family 'the bad news', Heidi came to my bedroom to tell me about the mountain that had blown. I felt another 'surge' (like mild electricity) of pulsating pain entering my right arm in the place where people develop a 'tennis elbow'. Then

Heidi stopped talking and was just starting with big eyes asking:" Are you ok, mama? You are white as a sheet!"

"I don't know," I answered, then I explained how my body felt, but Heidi just smiled and said;" The only way to find out is to get out of bed!

So, I did, but my body felt like a 'ten pounds of mud in a five-pound bag'! My right arm seemed as if it was made of iron, I could hardly lift it. On top of it all, my ears were ringing so bad that I could not hear anything!

Since that day, I have learned to register earthquakes deep within the earth around the earth. My healing went slowly forward and during this time I had plenty of time to learn of my 'newfound motion' surging through my body. I have learned that every day now, as I wake up, I ask for information from 'the powers that be' about what's happening around the earth. Lately, I'm in constant pain. I have one instance to share; During a very large murder investigation in Atlanta, GA. I saw, as if in a lightning flash, a person who I felt was the guilty party and was not the person in custody. My telepathy was so strong that I wrote to the police department in Atlanta to tell what I'd 'seen'. I received a letter back saying that I had not been the only one who had written with similar statements. Upon discovery of new evidence, the case was reopened and the outcome came as no surprise to me. I was right as they found the other person guilty!

After my 2nd surgery, my doctor said my days of cleaning houses were definitely over and suggested that I change occupations!

I thought of the counselor at the college and went to see him, who advised me to speak with a career counselor, who advised me to take some aptitude tests, which I did. The tests had 585 questions, which took most of two and a half hours to fulfill.

Two weeks later the results came back and the counselor said I had the interest and aptitude to become a chef and to work with the public.

I enrolled in the food service program at the college. As a part of a two-year curriculum, I worked part-time to earn credit hours. The first year in the program was an easy one for me. A small restaurant at the college, run by students under the teacher's supervision. During the first year, students in the food program work mainly in the kitchen or the dining room of this little restaurant.

The second year is mostly classroom and bookwork with no kitchen duties unless a special dinner or banquet popped up, then the most experienced students will assist in preparing the menu and food. After I received my degree and diploma in the spring of 1984, I decided to fly to Norway to visit my family. My father had been ailing and I was anxious to see him and my mother, my daughter Evy and her family, and if possible, my brother Sten. On April 29 1984, Wylie and Heidi drove me to Portland, where I caught the plane to Seattle, where I changed to my SAS plane bound for Copenhagen, Denmark. I had just stashed my bags away and sat down when the captain, accompanied by a stewardess, asked if my name was Randi McKinnon.

"Yes," I answered, wondering what was up with this!

"Would you come with me?" he said gruffly.

While the stewardess picked up my coat and bags, I grabbed my purse and followed the captain to first class, where I was issued a seat!

"Please forgive me for being so rough with you," he began," but I hate to see women traveling alone or without an escort!" So, for the duration of the flight, I sat in first class. Mealtime was a pure delight… We had champagne with the appetizer, two kinds of wine with dinner, and brandy with dessert! After the meal, the lights were dimmed and we were given socks for our feet, blankets, and pillows. It was nap time but I was much too excited to sleep. Here I was, flying first class 'rubbing elbows' with the rich and well-to-do, plus I was going home to see my family for the first time in eleven years! What more could a person wish for?

A man who was traveling business class, sat in the seat next to me. The week before he had been on business to Tokyo, Japan, and was now going back to Norway. He asked me what my life's ambitions were.

I told him of my degree and my dream to start a restaurant. He gave me pointers and ideas to expand on, then told me that his wife was divorcing him because she couldn't get used to his traveling. She wanted to live happily 'ever after' in a little house in the suburbs somewhere! The man sounded so lonely and bitter that I let him talk it all out! He asked if I like to keep him company during our two-and-a-half-hour layover at the Copenhagen airport while waiting for our flight to Norway and I gladly accepted his offer!

"Let's take a walk around the airport," He suggested. I was happy with the exercise after sitting in a chair for nine hours. Even in the reclining chairs in first class, it felt wonderful to walk and I took long steps.

"Hey, you'd better slow down or you're going to be very tired by the time we get to Norway!" Leon warned.

"I'm sorry, I didn't realize I was walking so fast, my body felt so stiff after the flight that it felt good to limber up!" I spoke.

We continued walking around the airport, but it started to feel like a maze and I quickly became mentally tired of all the stimulating sights. There were all kinds of bright-colored shops and lots of glass everywhere. When I listened closely, I could hear almost every language of the world being spoken. Finally, we sat down in a small cafe and ordered two coffees. Leon started talking about himself again. While I half-listened to his words which were flowing faster than a flowing stream, I thought how wonderful and exhausting traveling was. He interrupted my reverie with a few questions about myself. I told him that I was happily married and had been for nineteen years. Right now, I was heading for Northern Norway, to visit my ailing father and my mother, most likely for the last time. I also hoped to see the rest of the family as well.

Leon smiled as he listened to my story while tears filled his eyes.

"All the money in the world can't buy what you have! Your children, your family, and your own personal happiness that shines from your eyes make the picture complete," he said as he shook my hand.

Leon's kind words brought back a twenty-year-old ache that is deep in my heart and will never leave. I felt his pain- and all the money he was earning could not bring him happiness. All he really had to show for all his hard work, was an empty life of constant travel!

Soon it was time to board our flight to Oslo, Norway. It was Leon's final destination, but I still had other connections to make.

Another meal was served as soon as the plane was in the air and the seat belt sign was off. I could not eat a bite since I was still full from the huge meal we had on the overseas flight.

When we landed in Oslo, I was overcome with the emotions of being in 'my own country' again. Tears rolled down my cheeks when I heard the 'language of my youth'!

Leon broke my trance to wish me future happiness and I wished him the same. He squeezed my hand extra hard, then disappeared into the crowd and I didn't see him again. I claimed my luggage and was loading it on a cart when I heard my name over the P.A. system. Immediately, I started worrying that something had happened to my father but I couldn't find out what I was being paged for until I passed customs. When I finally got to the toll window and declared what I had brought with me, I asked the man to please hurry. He did his best and when he finished, I dashed to the information window. It was a message from Sten. He wanted me to alter my ticket so I could take an earlier flight and stop off at his town, where he would pick me up and take me to his home for about 45 minutes of chatting. What a super way to get to meet his family, even though the time would be short! I hustled to the ticket window and explained my plight. The agent said it would take 15 minutes to alter the ticket. While I waited, I began to notice how lethargic I felt; after all, I hadn't slept in 24 hours. But there was too much to look at so I had no trouble staying awake. After 15 min. had passed, I walked back to the ticket window and picked up my rescheduled ticket. Since I had another 2-hour wait, I checked my luggage, exchanged a few traveler's checks, and then bought a cup of coffee and a magazine to read. I didn't sit long at a time because the chairs had become very uncomfortable all of a sudden! I eavesdropped on conversations, especially two 5-year-old girls. They were trying to guess where people came from and where they were going. As far as they could tell, I was from Germany and was going to Ireland because I was wearing a parka! Finally, I couldn't hold my silence any longer.

"Are you sure of my destination"? I asked in my own dialect. They smiled shyly but did not speak. When I told them where I came from, their mouths dropped open in surprise as they said", If you come from America, how come you are not wearing a sundress instead of a parka"?

I told them that where I came from in America, have an early spring with cool weather. In fact," I added," When I left Seattle, it was a lot colder than Oslo, windy and rainy!"

The girls ran to the parents and excitedly told them of our conversation. We all ended up chatting about various subjects and my time lapsed fast, much to my enjoyment.

Before I knew it, the boarding call for my flight was announced. I bid the girls goodbyes and headed for the boarding gate. I was on a commuter with small uncomfortable seats. I'm so tired and probably will only be able to speak English, I thought because it now came much easier than Norwegian.

I found out that the crew knew where I came from and I was treated like 'royalty'. I looked out the window and took in the most breathtaking view I had experienced in a long time. We flew over miles and miles of lakes, forests, and mountains, along with grassy fields that looked like green postage stamps from the air. Then we flew over what the captain called 'The Alps of northern Norway'. These high snow-covered peaks were so jagged that they took my breath away! We flew so close to one peak, that it took my breath away! The captain told a folktale of how the peaks got so jagged. As the story went on, two trolls were fighting over a girl troll. While they rolled and skidded about, they pushed up great mounds of dirt and rocks with an awful fury, giving the mountains the jagged peaks they have today. The captain ended his story with;" And to our American guest, Welcome to northern Norway!"

I was flattered and when one of the stewardesses came by, I asked her to thank the captain for his kindness and tell him that I was returning home to visit my family after 11 years of absence. We were close enough to the town where my brother lived. It's a lovely little town of 50,000 people nestled by the ocean. A large jetty shields the town from the sometimes-violent North Sea. A sea inlet divides the town in half and a large bridge links the town together.

Then something caught my eye.

Oh my gosh, I thought, we are going to land on the ocean! I couldn't see any runway. The water came closer and closer and I still couldn't see the runway

I looked again and then suddenly- I saw the shoreline and knew -with relief that it had to be the runway appearing. The plane landed safely and I sent up a prayer of thanks. I gathered up my purse and hand luggage, made sure I had my ticket ready, and walked out into the sunshine. As I walked into the waiting room, someone yelled: "Auntie Randi"! And I had two little arms around my neck. It was my little niece Sissel, A skinny girl with dark blond hair, a big smile, and the darkest brown eyes. Behind her stood her brother Stian, a tall lanky boy with the same features as his sister except for the smile – he was shy. I coached him to me and got hug number 2. Then came my tears as I got the 3rd hug. My brother Sten doesn't let emotions show, however, this time he cleared his throat several times as he mumbled we'd better get going as his wife had dinner ready at his house. While en route to Sten's house, the kids chatted along about their interests. Sten and I spoke about my trip, the weather, and his wife Sylvia, who was 6 months pregnant.

I enjoyed the drive through my old stomping grounds in this town where I met Einar, even though I didn't get to see the downtown, just the outside perimeter.

We arrived at the house and his pretty wife greeted us at the door. She's a petite lady with a shy smile and delicate features. Despite being 6 months pregnant, she moved about with ease and grace.

She had prepared a most delicious meal of reindeer meat, potatoes, and vegetables, and for dessert, chocolate pudding with custard sauce followed by coffee and brandy. I gave the children their gifts but what pleased them the most was the bubblegum I gave them. Soon my time was up and my brother drove me to the airport for the last leg of my journey to Kirkenes, where the rest of my family lived. While sitting in the plane waiting for the 'take off', I reflected on how little I knew my little brother and his family even less. I hoped I would get to know them better in the future. The last 'leg' of my journey took 'an eternity' it seemed! Looking out over the landscape, I saw rolling hills, snow, and valleys- all in shades of white, grey, and brown. The only really beautiful sight was the sunset and it was incredible! I had forgotten about the Finnmark sun and its beauty, and just the sight of it gave me a lump in my throat- the shades of tinted orange with pink and red were so exquisite that even the most talented painter would have trouble duplicating such beauty, I'm fairly certain of.

As we neared Kirkenes, I had little 'butterflies' stirring my stomach. I was eagerly waiting to see my mother again. To be alone with her and have long talks like we used to do. I was also anxious to see my father and hoped and prayed that he would recognize me. But now, I was close to the point of exhaustion as I hadn't slept in 36 hours! The plane prepared for landing and was gliding onto the runway and came to a stop. My 'butterflies' were going crazy- would my mother approve of the way I looked now, I wondered. Ever since I was a young girl, I had tried to assure her approval, but rarely received a word or even a gesture from her. I hoped it would be different this time!

When the door of the plane opened, a cold breeze blew in! I thought, so typical of Kirkenes, hence its nickname- "The Drafty City"! I walked down the stairs and across the tarmac toward the terminal. Outside the door stood Mama, dressed in a brown coat and wearing a scarf on her head. Her glasses seemed too big for her narrow face. In fact, her whole body seemed tinier than the last time I saw her, eleven years ago. That was after she had weight reduction surgery. Her doctors had given her six mo. of life if she didn't do something about her weight. Her problem had started in her childhood because she was born with both hips out of joint but at that time, there were no surgeries to correct the condition. She became a professional tailor; this didn't require much standing or walking. Then she fell in love with my father and married him at the tender age of 18 years old.

As far back as I could remember, she had always been what was called 'pleasingly plump' but after giving birth to my first brother (Who died), and my present brother, she gained a lot of weight and her legs refused to carry her and she resorted to an office chair with rollers and she rolled around the house. More trouble arrived when she developed arthritis in all her joints. Long story shortened – she had her surgery and lost the allotted weight but she was wrinkled but I didn't care, It's my mama. But I saw tears in her eyes as I hugged her gently but my wise mama soon smiled and got to business…

"Why are we crying?" she asked," this is a happy occasion! Let's gather your luggage, take a taxi home, and have some coffee!"

Just the thought of food made my stomach flip-flop! Oh-no-not again, the stomach moaned- no more food!

Mama had a taxi waiting and the driver grabbed my luggage and we were off to Mama's apartment. While we drove through the snow-decked landscape, dotted with a few trees, mama wanted to know if I recognized certain places but I had to admit that I did not. She was disappointed as I could tell but after all, it had been almost 30 years since I had been in that section of town.

One thing I was never good at, was reading my mama's face for she had what's called a poker face'. When she was sad or angry, she didn't speak. But when she was happy, the only way to tell was to look at her tiny feet, they were usually tapping out some rhythmic music known only to her. The poker face was passed down to my uncle, mama's brother and I imagine they both 'got it' from my Grandma, Kristine.

We arrived at the apartment, and walking in the door and seeing the items I grew up with was a lot and tears fell but I didn't let Mama see that because she would have had something to say about it!

She made herself busy in the kitchen making coffee and something to go with the coffee, maybe bread and cheese. I changed into something more comfortable. I hoped my words- most of them anyway, would make sense to her. Mama had a high IQ and was very good at interpreting unusual-sounding sentences. If she didn't understand, she would paraphrase or talk around it until she understood. Our evening went like this and we talked and laughed until I started to feel lightheaded and said that I had to go to bed and said how many hours I had been awake. She drew her eyebrows down as she said; "So put yourself to bed already!"

I kissed and hugged her and said I loved her- then I went to bed.

The next morning, I awoke when Mama stirred in the bed next to mine. It was only 6;30 and Mama wanted me to go back to bed but I was completely rested and I knew it was the pollution-free air in the area that had all to do with me being so rested.

I stood up from the bed and dressed in front of the open window. Mama shook her head at her 'crazy daughter' who was dressing in front of an open window with cold air coming in and said:" What are you doing?" When I told her of my hay fever and the wonderful Kirkenes air, she looked at me with a sobering face and said:" Too bad you can't pack up a couple of bags of air and take them with you when you leave!"

We had breakfast, then she suggested we should go to visit Papa at the hospital's geriatrics ward. She phoned for a taxi to pick us up. This was a stretch of road I could easily walk in 15 minutes but she couldn't walk that far. When we walked into the visiting room, a nurse wheeled Papa in from his room. Mama explained to him that she was a bit early because she had brought a guest.

"Do you recognize this lady?" she asked.

"Evy?" he asked.

"No, not Evy," Mama said, "Think hard about the past."

All of a sudden, he broke into loud crying and Mama asked who I was again.

"Randi," he said as I put my arms around him, kissed him, and held him as both of us cried together. The silver-haired man I was holding in my arms, was just a shell of his former self. How could I have denied his fatherly love for all that time? I knew now that I loved him with all my heart!!

Papa was always a little stiff and unyielding and didn't like to give hugs. One would never catch him kissing anyone on the cheek. Now he just sat leaning on me crying! When the tears subsided, he wanted to know all about me and my family in America. I hurried to tell before he forgot who I was. Then he abruptly changed the subject and began to ask Mama questions unrelated to the past. As they talked, I studied his face thinking how terribly old he had gotten in those last eleven years. The stroke he suffered had left him with a puffy face and a paralyzed left side and he still complained of a lot of pain on the left side, from the top of his head to the tip of his toes. I loved him so much at that moment that my chest wanted to explode! This man had always been a peaceful and serene man and of very few words but now he lived among constant commotion! It happens a lot in some rest homes, the geriatrics ward is short-staffed. Many of the patients are ignored or forgotten. These become starved for visitors or somebody to speak with or to just sit next to.

One day when I came to visit Papa alone while Mama stayed at home. The nurses hadn't finished their morning routine so I had to wait a while. I noticed a tall, slim and very pretty lady in her early 50s sitting in a wheelchair in the parlor. She motioned me to come to her and I discovered she couldn't speak. She wanted for me to wheel her out to the foyer to the newsstand where she could buy cigarettes. I asked her to wait while I asked a nurse for permission to wheel her there. The nurse gave her OK and I wheeled her out to the foyer. She was so grateful and thanked me over and over. After that day, she made everybody notice me and she gestured to everyone, her signs to the fact of what I did to help her.

One day mama wanted to know what she was trying to tell her, I told her about my good deed, and Mama smiled and shook her head at the commotion.

The days rolled by too fast and then the two weeks were gone and I was to take the bus to my home village to spend time with Evy and her family.

Most of my Norwegian had come back, even the dialect, although I would get stuck on words, which is normal for the circumstances!

I had to take a 3-HR bus ride to the village where she lived. I didn't recognize any of the other passengers who came on the bus after me were from the village where I grew up. These spoke Finnish among themselves as the village was settled by Finns some 120 years before then. One woman who's an aunt to a girl who was part of the circle of friends that I belonged to, came to me and asked: "Excuse me for being forward but is your name Randi?" I said 'yes' and it was nice to talk and the tour went really quickly. Then suddenly, she turned to her friends and spoke Finnish again and I thought; 'how typical of them- nothing has changed'. I listened to others speak around me and I heard The Sami language as well which I love very much but have never been able to learn. Since I have Laplander blood surging in my veins, it is part of my heritage and which I'm very proud to proclaim I have!

Back to the bus ride…

The bus sped on through the turns and bumps of the road. I looked at the landscape covered with boulders, hills, and snow that was melting quickly in the spring sun. My eyes filled with tears as I remembered how much I had missed this part of Norway and I was glad that I had my sunglasses on so the rest of the passengers wouldn't see my tears. Then they would really have something to gossip about, wouldn't they?

When we came closer to the little place where Evy lived, I asked the driver to stop when we arrived at the stop at the little village. We drove around a few more bends in the road. Around the next bend, I saw a few houses, then I saw a little girl standing by the road waving her little arms and jumping up and down as if there was a trampoline. The bus stopped and the driver said: "You have finally arrived!" He helped with the luggage, then the bus drove off again!

Behind the first little girl stood an identical girl and I knew they were my granddaughters, Fanny and Helen. I got down on my knees and hugged the girls, then we laughed and hugged again. I heard someone calling 'mama, mama' and I knew that voice anywhere and turned to look. There came Evy, half running, half walking, wheeling a baby buggy with her youngest child, a boy named Dann. She was crying and we hugged, cried, and laughed. She piled my luggage onto the baby buggy and we walked the 5 minutes to their house. Their house was very nice but small but very cozy and perfect for this little family. The colors were amazing in hues of burnt cinnamon, natural fir, warm yellow, and white. The sun shone through the big bay windows in the living room since shading draperies don't exist in too many of the houses in Finnmark. The people try to capture the sun as much as possible, while it lasts. The day I arrived; the sun really put on a show. There was not a cloud in the sky and no gusts of wind either- in fact- it was balmy!

The little district where Evy lived were houses built by the government and low-income housing but they really didn't look like low-income housing! They were well-kept and pretty but very cold in winter, according to Evy. After the children and I spent some time together, she sent the girls out to play and put the baby down for a nap. Then she made coffee and she and I talked for a while. At first, we both felt a little awkward, but that gradually disappeared!

Evy and I hadn't spoken since she came to live with us at Hamar in 1974. She was just a teenager then, trying to find herself without help from anybody, the least of all me- her mother. To be candid- she didn't actually know me and I don't know but my feeling was that she didn't WANT to know of me! When we said our 'goodbye' then, she seemed 'happy' that I was going back to the USA. At that time, Evy was a petite young lady with naturally curly hair and a pearly white smile. Her husband Leif, spent the week as an arc welder repairing large equipment at a big iron ore company in Kirkenes. He'd leave for work on Sun evening and come home on Saturday afternoon. Since Leif was gone all week, I had a good chance to get to know my daughter and her children before he returned on Saturday. Deep down, I wasn't ready to meet my son-in-law, MY son-in-law!!

My granddaughters, Fanny and Helen, were beautiful twins, at least in my grandmotherly eyes! Their lovely brown eyes hid all kinds of mischief and love for each other. Their little brother Dann had the same color eyes and the same smile as his sisters. He wasn't walking yet and unfortunately- I didn't get to see him take his first step, a grandmother's dream come true!!

Evy and I spoke a lot about the past. We discussed WHY I had to leave her with Mama and WHY I didn't send for her while I lived in the USA. Some interesting information came to light suddenly... When I told her that Wylie and I had written a letter to Mama and asked for her. Mama answered that she had a medical situation where she had to stay in Norway for her doctor's care. I was floored as I listened to her telling me that it was not true- I had never had a problem such as that! All the while during her explanation, her tears were flowing and so was mine in pure helplessness and we ended up sitting and holding each other crying! It was truly a release for both of us! When we stopped crying, we turned and looked at each other and burst into laughter at the sight. Our noses were running and our faces were streaked with tears. We cleaned up and Evy made coffee and found that we had FINALLY run out of conversation on our subject but as women and mother-daughter- we NEVER ran out of things to talk about- and felt that there was so much to be said!! We had truly cleared the road as it were!

While I was there, we walked to the village where we both grew up, a brisk 20-minute walk. The village sits on a sand spit that emerged from the ocean more than 1300 years ago and the ocean is now slowly reclaiming the land. The population has changed a great deal since I lived there. From the 1960s and forward, the pop. Have gone from over 1000 to barely 700 now. The only industry there is a fish packing plant and I don't know how it's doing now but at that time I was there, the plant was 'holding its own'.

It was nice to meet some of the people in the village and notice how aged they had become. Many women my age looked twice as old!

While there, I had a chance to celebrate Norway's Independence Day which is on May 17th and is called THE CHILDREN'S DAY because children are celebrated on that day. They can do anything within reason, and get away with it!

On May 16th at 3;30 AM a parade came through the streets, waking people out of their sleep by beating on aluminum with ladles, etc., and yelling Hurrah, hurrah may 17 is here! This usually is done by high schoolers sneaking alcohol from somewhere and the police usually don't do anything unless the law's broken. They let the 'kids' blow off steam! At 10 AM one shows up for the very large parade with marching bands, dressed in national costumes and carrying Norway's small flags. Evy, the children, and I joined the parade. I had bought the girls identical outfits and a suit for the baby boy who rode in the stroller watching with big eyes.

Later that evening, the entertainment committee put on a dance, and Evy wanted to know if I was up to going- I said -of course!!

Leif had the flu and babysat the kids and said for us to go to the dance so we did. I drove Leif's car to the dance. When I walked in the door, it was like stepping back in time… The men were standing in a small circle outside the hall and I knew right away what they were doing, they were 'passing the bottle'. Inside the women of all ages were sitting at small tables, drinking coffee and soft drinks and gossiping while listening to the hired dance band. I sat with the women of my age, several of whom were my classmates from school. Before long, I was asked to dance, and from then on- I was on my feet. The younger men discovered I could dance the up-to-date dances, so they asked me to dance every dance. I got tired fast but I had a lot of fun because dancing is something I really enjoy. Then the band played the closing piece of music and We left. When we sat in the car Evy let out a yell and slapped her knees. "What are you doing?" I asked, wide-eyed in surprise.

"All the people I was sitting with were green with envy when they saw me walk in with you, mama, she said. "They said you looked so pretty and young compared to their mothers, who wear their hair in a bun and never use makeup. They are so frumpy looking, compared to you. They wouldn't be caught 'dead' on the dance floor doing modern dances. I'm so proud of you, mama!!" She reached over and gave me a big 'bear hug'. Driving back to the house, I smiled thinking about how I had finally triumphed – And I had fun without going overboard!!

The following day I was to leave and go back to the USA.

The girls cried, and I felt terribly sad as well! We all had just gotten to know each other and now I had to leave for how long- nobody knew for sure!

Chapter 11

On Sunday morning, we had breakfast then Leif drove us to Kirkenes and when we arrived at Mama's house, she acted extremely nervous for some reason, most likely me leaving Norway that day. I didn't say anything but Mama let her nervousness out in the open and started nagging and Evy especially, caught her sharp tongue! I felt so badly, being in the middle like that but what could I have said without making matters worse? Since it was my last day there, I didn't want to say anything that could have made matters worse and caused deep wounds that would never have healed. I also had the feeling that I would not see Mama alive ever again, so I kept my mouth shut. Evy burst into tears and my heart ached for her, thinking how much harmony, laughter, and happiness we achieved at her house and reminded her of it and she started feeling better right away.

My little family stayed overnight at Mama's, and then the next day Evy, the girls, and I walked to the hospital to visit Papa. He seemed happy to see us and recognized all of us and in his quiet humorous way, joked with us. I asked Evy and the girls not to say that I was leaving because I was afraid it would hurt him but we also knew he would forget the minute we were out of sight.

Evy and the girls stayed with Papa for a moment to give me time to collect myself, then we walked back to Mama's place. She had lunch ready when we walked in. When we finished, I started packing. Then it was time to leave for the airport. Evy and family were seeing me off, mama didn't want to come. While I said my 'goodbye' to Mama, Leif carried my luggage to the car. It was very tearful for me but Mama was not for 'flowery words,' so her s was a light squeeze and a tear or two. Since I usually carry my heart on my sleeve, I tried to tell her how much I loved her and how I wished we lived closer to visit more often. But to all this, I got no answers and let it go at that. I gave her one last kiss and with tears streaming down my face I left. On the way to the airport, everyone was quiet and arriving there, I quickly checked my luggage. We went to the coffee shop to wait for my departure time. I thanked Leif for putting up with his mother-in-law for two weeks and for letting me enjoy his little family. He didn't answer, just smiled as he looked down at his hands. The speaker's voice told me my departure and we said our 'bye's. I hugged Leif- much to his embarrassment, then I hugged and kissed the children. The girls cried and hugged my waist saying: "We don't want you to leave, we love you, Grandma!"

"We will meet again girls, as soon as God will let us," I said and hugged them back.

Dann gave me kisses and reached out and with one finger, touched one tear and said: "M-ma cry?"

Then it was time to say 'bye' to Evy and we both collapsed in tears.

"I finally know you for what you are, mama," she began," You're a loving mother and grandmother, but our time, this time, was much too short! I love you, Mama!"

My heart was singing with joy from her words. As tears were streaming down my face, I told her what she meant to me in all those years I hadn't seen her.

"You are my firstborn, my love," I started, "You almost died as a baby, and by that, you became very special to me, and you always will be!" With those parting words, I walked toward the plane and boarded. I found my window seat and looked out and there, by the fence stood a lonely figure, looking toward the plane. As the plane lifted off the ground, I tried to relax and meditate but to no avail. My mind was spinning with faces, and Evy's crying face kept coming back again and again.

While I was at Evy's house, Sten called Mama to ask me to stop again on my return flight and have a talk again. When the plane landed, he and the children were waiting for me and off to the coffee shop until it was time for me to leave again. Saying 'bye' to my brother is usually a formal affair with little or no affection, not even to his sister whom he hadn't seen in 11 years. When we hugged Sten turned the back of his head to me, the way he used to do as a child. But I said my greeting as best I could, hugged and kissed the children. Sissel jumped and locked her legs around my waist and said she wanted me to stay. I kissed her and she let go. Stian was very shy, so I had to go to him and get my hug and kiss while he giggled a lot, and then I had to go. While walking toward the plane, I stopped and saw them waiving and waiving back. I stayed in Oslo for 2 days and so I explored the town a bit. Since I was alone, I had to be careful and not stray too far from my hotel, which I didn't but I visited many small bistros and coffee shops.

In the morning, I was leaving, it poured rain as an appropriate Bon Voyage! As I boarded the plane bound for Denmark, I started getting a headache. Since I can't take remedies for it because I often have a severe allergic reaction to it, I knew that I was in trouble.

The next 9 hours would seem like an eternity and be a nightmare for me!

We landed in Denmark and I would have loved to go into town but with that headache no, no! I was sitting feeling sorry for myself when a very stately lady sat down next to me. She said she was on her way to Seattle for her yearly visit with her daughter and family. This would be her 18th trip across the ocean from Sweden and said she was finding it harder and harder to do and said she was 85 years old.

"You certainly don't look your age," I said.

"Life has been good to me," she said and smiled.

By the time we reached Seattle, I really felt sick.

My headache had become so intense that it was real work to bend over or turn my head. My chest felt so tight and my throat sandpaper. The stewardess kept checking and giving me liquids to drink. I started to wonder what I might have contracted on my journey. I made my way through the customs in a daze and don't recall much of it. The officer was very sympathetic: "If you don't mind me saying so, you look terrible!"

"Gee, thanks, I needed that"! I said and smiled a weak smile.

Finally, my connecting flight left for my final destination Portland, where Wylie would be waiting for me. I almost cried when I saw him standing there smiling.

We hugged and I said; "I'm sorry, I can't kiss you, I have a bug or some kind of virus I picked up somewhere.

He gave me an extra squeeze, then smiled that good smile of his, took my hand and we were off to retrieve my luggage.

At last, I thought to Eugene to peace and quiet, I thought. Little did I know how this evening was going to end.

On the way home, Wylie made small talk and suggested that we'd stop for dinner, which we did. I wasn't really hungry, all I wanted was to take a long nap. After we ate, we still had to drive an hour down the valley before we reached Eugene.

I settled back and tried to enjoy the drive and my husband and reflect on what had occurred during the last month, but I felt uneasy and I didn't know why, so I chalked it up to 'jet lag'.

Then Wylie started telling me about a phone call he had received while I was away. It was a woman from California, and she seemed to know too many details about my past life and my first husband to be a prank caller, he said.

"Would you happen to know what she's talking about"?

I went cold all over and suddenly saw my whole past race by. Evy had predicted that it would be just a matter of time before we heard from her sister Katie, how right she was!

"I can't really concentrate right now to figure it out, Wylie," I said. Then I changed the subject, "Will Heidi be home when we get there?"

He said that he had asked her to be there and we hoped her boyfriend wouldn't be there because neither one of us liked him very much.

When we arrived home, who would be there but Heidi and her boyfriend? I politely asked him to leave but he resisted and looked at Heidi for support. She took the hint and said that my homecoming was for family only, and he finally left!

Then she started talking about the phone calls from a lady in California. The more she talked about the calls, the more upset she became. Finally, I decided to take a stand.

"Sit down, both of you, I have a story to tell you but I want you both to listen without interrupting me. When I finished talking, Heidi came to me and put her arms around me and we both cried. She asked me to forgive her rudeness and insensitivity on the matter. Wylie, on the other hand, was pacing the floor in anger!

"Wylie, please speak to me," I pleaded. He whirled to look at me.

"Why haven't you said anything about this during all the years of marriage?" he demanded to know.

"I was bound by a piece of paper that I signed at the time," I told him. "I've been living in a private hell all these years that I still haven't been released from!"

He came and put his arms around Heidi and me. There we stood in the middle of the living room floor, and my tears finally released me from my private hell. When I finished, I opened my suitcases and gave them the presents I had bought in Norway for each of them.

"Do you feel like going out for dessert?" Heidi asked. "I didn't have a chance to make anything for your homecoming."

We had our dessert at the pie shop and came home and I went straight to bed. Long before he did. He said that when he came to bed, I stirred and said something in Norwegian to him which he understood. I said 'It's good to be home'. He answered' That's good' in English.

That following afternoon the phone rang and I answered.

"Are you Randi?" a light female voice said.

"Yes," I answered.

"This is your daughter, Katie," the woman began," I want you to know, I don't blame you in any way for what you had to do. I just want to hear from you why you had to adopt my brother and me." With tears streaming down my face, I told her the whole story. When I finished, the line was quiet for a moment, then I heard a sniffle. Katie cleared her voice and said, "Now I know the whole story."

She continued to tell me that she had spent the last 11 years looking for me trying to find me. Katie had tried agencies that specialize in matters such as these, but they wanted too much money and too much paperwork. Finally, her mother suggested that she try a friend of theirs, who said she knew where I lived. All Katie had to do then was to call the phone company to get my number.

"I've been nervous since I first called your home," she admitted. "I was so afraid that you wouldn't talk to me. When you did, I had a release of nerves and shook like a leaf. We made small talk for 45 minutes, then she hung up. After I hung up, I had to sit to compose myself. My knees had turned to jelly and my heart was pounding so hard that I knew everyone could hear it. I was still crying but with joy. My prayers will finally be answered soon, I thought. I'm going to see my children again and I started to daydream about the last meeting. All through 1984 and into the spring of 1985, Katie and I kept in touch by phone. A couple of times I even spoke with my son John but he doesn't acknowledge me as his mother. Even though I understand his feelings, it still hurts deep down in my soul. When the adoption took place, he was only 9 months old, so how could he possibly remember me at all? Katie was 4 years old, so she did remember me.

In the spring of 1985, Wylie suggested that we drive down to Davis, CA to visit his father. Then drive to Clovis to visit Katie and hopefully see John. I was so thrilled when he made the suggestion, and asked why he did.

"I've become curious about Katie and John," he said, "I wanted to meet them. I have a family that's growing bigger day by day!"

146

We drove to CA, but this time the trip was somehow different from all the other trips we had made over the years. There was a certain lighthearted air about us as we made our way south. We talked about Katie and John and all that had happened during the last year openly, and it felt so good to not have anything hidden anymore.

"Let us not talk to Dad about the reason we're going to Clovis," I suggested and he agreed. We were afraid it might upset Dad.

Wylie's dad was a gentle, soft-spoken man in his 90s. Since Wylie's mom died of cancer four years prior, he had lived alone in their two-bedroom apartment in a complex that he co-managed. Besides cooking and cleaning for himself, he also goes on bicycle jaunts around the complex! I had a special place in my heart for Dad, as I called him because he was so different from Wylie's mom. Throughout the years, I had to earn her trust and love and even though I loved her just as much as I loved Dad, it was in a different way.

We stayed with Dad two days before we said that we were driving to Clovis to visit some friends. We arrived at Katie's house around 1;30 PM. Her house was ranch style, half brick, half wood with rose bushes everywhere!

We rang the doorbell, the door opened wide and there stood my daughter, the prettiest woman I had seen in a long time, with whitish hair, sky blue eyes that sparkled with mischief, and a big open smile!

We embraced and cried and for a moment- it was just Katie and I in the whole Universe! My heart was beating so hard I thought it would explode!

All of a sudden, I remembered Wylie, who had been standing discreetly behind me. I introduced them to each other, a little embarrassed about forgetting him.

For the first few hours, I didn't even notice anything about the décor, I only saw Katie. I wanted to absorb all the years of her youth that I had missed. In my heart, I hoped John would come by or call but he did neither. I did have a chance to speak with him by phone and got a real shock, his voice and choice of words are the true image of his father. It was just as if I spoke with Einar and I said that and he was still for a moment.

When Katie and I first embraced, she said something that she had to explain right away. "I always remember the smell of your hair and now I smell it again. When I was a little girl, whenever I met another woman, I would find some excuse to smell their hair but it was always the wrong smell!"

Wylie and I had a lovely time the two days we spent with Katie. She didn't have room for us to stay overnight so we stayed in a motel. The second evening at the motel, I asked his opinion of her and he thought she was a lovely young lady but then he put his arms around me as he said;" How you must have suffered all these years not knowing the welfare of your children!"

At that moment, I felt total fulfillment and I knew that he finally understood. The only drawback to the visit with Katie was the heat. Hot weather and I do not get along- never have- never will! When the temperature climbs, my body inevitably fills with fluids, which happened in Clovis but it was worth it to get to see my girl! When it was time to leave, we said a tearful 'goodbye', promising to see each other as soon as possible!

It was a hot 5 hour drive up the valley to Davis and the air conditioning felt wonderful! I took a shower and changed clothes and was my old self again. Dad suggested we go out to eat and I didn't mind at all!

That evening we decided to tell Dad what we were doing in Clovis. He wasn't at all surprised. "Oh well, there are never enough grandchildren to please a grandpa's heart," he said.

I thought that it was very gracious of him and said so!

After Wylie and I went to bed, he put his arms around me and gave me a squeeze as he said: "You know, all of a sudden, everything is beginning to make sense. About two months before we were married, Aunt Nell (Grandma Martha's sister) said to me that from now on you need extra amounts of tender loving care. At the time, I didn't understand what she meant. Maybe it was because we were in love and were getting married, plus the fact that you didn't have any of your family here." He took a breath and then continued, "Now it makes sense. It was the loss of your children she was talking about. What a living hell you must have been through all these years. No wonder you had two ulcers.

He stared out into space, then he continued: "I know what we'll do. Let's start driving homeward a day early. I will have a surprise for you!"

I tried to sweet-talk the surprise from him but he was tight-lipped.

The following morning, we stood up at 6:30 and had breakfast with Dad. Then we said 'goodbye which was always difficult to do when leaving Dad. He always looked so lost and sad and I often caught myself wondering if that would be the last time we saw him alive because I loved him as if he were my own father.

As we drove up the valley toward the Oregon border, I became more curious by the minute, but I decided to hold my tongue, while we drove past Weed and headed for Yreka. "Let's stop in Yreka for the night?" he suggested, "As soon as we have checked in, we'll head down the valley toward Thompson Creek where you used to live, ok?" I was so surprised and elated tears came as I thanked him for his idea. The place on Thompson Creek that Grandma Martha used to own had changed a lot since last I saw it.

The caretaker's cottage where I and my little family used to live was still as pretty as before. The wood stove I used for bread baking was gone. The cottage had been modernized totally on the inside for tourism and the charm was gone.

Grandma Martha's Garden with the 10000 bulbs, was now a swimming pool area. I chatted with the owner, who was the second owner since Grandma Martha owned the place. The owner was pleased to hear about the way it used to look, at least she acted as if she were. After one more look, we said 'goodbye' and headed back to Yreka. We had dinner at a restaurant, but I lost it all when we got back to the motel room! I could not tell if it was the excitement I had had over the past few days or the food we had. That evening it was my turn to put my arm around my man and thank him for all he had done for me on our trip. For a lot of men, going from having one daughter to a 'ready-made' family would have made them angry enough to seek a divorce.

"Oh no, you are stuck with me!" he said with that special twinkle in his eyes. My stomach continued to hurt and I didn't get much sleep that night. The next morning, I stood up early and showered, which made me feel a bit better. We had breakfast and started our drive back toward Oregon.

While we were away, Heidi had been our 'caretaker,' and took care of our house, cat, and dog. The house was clean and neat and she had done a terrific job and as her reward, we took her out to dinner.

She was eager to find out how the trip went and we gave her all the details. She assured us she was not jealous of Katie and we in return, said it was alright if she was jealous. After all, she was an only child who used to have her mama and Papa totally to herself. Suddenly, she's called upon to share her parents with a brother and two sisters! She just didn't know how to handle that and it took her breath away! Although she put on a brave front in front of Wylie and me, her friends told us she was upset about the situation.

"Imagine, I have a brother and a sister as close as California and all this time, I thought that I was an only child"!

Before Katie and John came into the picture, Heidi never regarded Evy as her sister, particularly since she hadn't seen her since she was 7 years old. Now 'things' were different in every way possible.

We had been home a little more than three weeks when we decided to invite Katie to visit Eugene. We sent her money for the train ticket, and she arrived at the end of June. On Monday, I made my usual visit to the spa but I cut it short because my left leg really hurt but didn't say anything to anyone when I came home. Heidi was always 'tuned' into me. When I was cleaning my spa clothes away, she came and grabbed my arm and said:" Ok, out with it, what's wrong?"

I told her what was going on and she 'ordered' me to call the doctor the next morning and she would drive me there! 'I don't want to hear you say no', she continued. Tuesday, I called the doctor, who said to come into his office, when he had examined me, he said; "Be at the hospital at 7 AM tomorrow to be admitted. I knew it would be just a matter of time before the disc herniated, we will operate immediately!"

Wylie and I packed my things as quietly as possible, as we backed out of the driveway, Katie's worried face peeked out of the bedroom window, and I waved and blew her a kiss.

We went in through the emergency entrance, where I was admitted right away and sent to my room in a wheelchair. After a 2-hour wait, I had a Myelogram, then at 2 PM, I had the surgery.

The following day, Katie, Heidi, and Wylie came to visit. Poor Katie, she was so shaken up to see me in the hospital, none of us figured her visit would turn out this way, least of all her!

I stayed in the hospital until the following Monday.

Since she had to leave early Sunday AM, she came to say 'goodbye' on Saturday.

I felt bad for her, but there was nothing I could have done as this was an emergency surgery. Heidi stayed home for three weeks to care for me, then she went to Salem to visit her boyfriend. I was a bit upset and felt that I could have used her a little longer.

Wylie was home in the morning at least and after he left for work, I did as little as possible.

While Heidi was in Salem, the mercury rose to 100*- which was expected since it was July. We didn't have air conditioning, so I became very hot and had an awful headache. To make myself comfortable, I took a cool shower, changed my clothes, then stretched out on the bed with my incision toward the open window and fell asleep.

The following day, I called the doctor and told him what happened.

He gave me a lecture saying: "You came dangerously close to a heatstroke! Never let that happen again. If you get that hot in the future, go straight to the emergency room. Your body is still too weak to ward off such extreme temperature changes.

As soon as the doctor released me, I started exercising very diligently three times each week, and soon I got my strength back, and soon after, everything fell into place!

In September 1985, Heidi flew to Miami for an 11-week course to learn computerized ticketing at an airline school. One week after she returned home, she moved to Portland. I missed her terribly for the first two months but I knew it was time for her to make her move, my little girl had grown up!

By the end of November, I had found something else to think about.

I started to feel bloated all the time, just like I used to feel when I was pregnant. Only this time, I knew it was medically impossible. The bloating continued for another three weeks before I saw my family physician, who sent me to a gynecologist. He had a scan done that found a 5 by 7-inch growth. Since it was close to Christmas, the doctor urged me to wait until after New Year. So, on January 3rd, I was admitted to the hospital AGAIN and that afternoon, I had surgery and the surgeon found 4 more growths that collectively weighed 11 pounds. All of them were benign, 'Thank goodness'! After the latest ordeal, I made myself a promise no more hospital stays! Toward the end of the year, Heidi decided to move back to Eugene to find work there. She discovered she could live at home cheaper than away. We liked the idea of having her home again. She found a job in security at the airport right away. A few weeks after she started her new job, she mentioned a certain young man she had met. Could she bring him home to meet us one evening? We encouraged her to do so. A few nights later, she brought him home. Jeff was tall and husky, wore glasses, and had a shy, but open smile. He spoke in a quiet way and we liked him right away. When I mentioned later to her that she'd made a good choice, she beamed happily. One evening close before the holidays, Heidi and Jeff asked to speak with us and said they had something important to tell us. Wylie and I had an 'idea' of what it might be. Heidi started the conversation, then Jeff took over.

"Heidi and I have decided to become engaged," he began, "and would like to get married next year," in August.

Wylie and I looked at each other first. My eyes begged him to say something before the silence became deafening, finally, he spoke.

"A bit sudden, isn't it?"

"Yes, it is actually," Jeff answered and his face turned red as he looked sideways at Heidi.

"Are you pregnant Heidi?" he asked her.

"No, Papa, I am not," she answered.

"We haven't made any commitments to each other but we like each other and we want to stay together for a while," Jeff said as he took Heidi's hand and she looked at him and smiled. The holidays came and went, as Wylie and I grew to like Jeff a lot.

In January, they decided to set the wedding date. Heidi met her future mother-in-law and said she liked her right away but got a 'cold shoulder' back in return.

A few weeks later Jeff told his mother that he planned to marry Heidi. His mother became very angry and threw him out of the house! Heidi asked us if he could move in with us and after thinking it over, we decided right away that it would be alright for him to do it! Then Heidi brought Jeff over to discuss the situation and as we talked, Jeff became very embarrassed.

"I just think it's wrong to live together before marriage," he tried to explain.

I tried to think of something to say that would ease his mind.

"Do you have any money, Jeff?" I asked. He had mentioned that he might have to live in a motel until he could make other arrangements.

"No, not really," He answered.

"Then stop and think for a minute about what I'm saying, Jeff. Wylie and I are offering you a place to stay. You can pay us whatever you can afford when you can afford it. You don't have to live with Heidi in her room, we do have an extra room where you can sleep."

After thinking it over, Jeff agreed to move in. Heidi told us later that Jeff wasn't used to having family members caring openly about each other as our family does. She also shared with us that Jeff had been taken away from his real mother at a very early age and reared by his grandmother, a stern woman who lived a hard life doing farm work. Her love for Jeff was never shown by tenderness but by material things. At the time Heidi met Jeff, he was a student at the university and had one term left to graduate. When the winter term began, Jeff did not sign up because he did not have the $1000 for tuition. As winter turned into spring, we began to make plans for Heidi and Jeff's wedding, which was to take place on August 15th.

Jeff thought he should pay for most of the expenses, so I called a family meeting on the matter. Wylie and I tried to explain to Jeff that we don't do things that way at our house. Since Jeff did not earn a great deal of money, he should let us help. Jeff's argument was that we were doing enough already by letting them use the house and yard for the reception. We finally agreed to split expenses 50-50!

But Wylie and I paid for little things here and there because we wanted to do it.

As the wedding date approached quickly, I started to panic because I couldn't get anything done! I Contracted a fellow chef to do the cooking and be in charge of the kitchen in general. Jim (the chef) noticed how frazzled I looked, so he asked if he could take complete charge and purchase all food and drink, which would give me extra time for the other important things that needed to be done. I accepted his offer gladly. I knew this man from the college where we went to cooking school together and we were a bit older than most of the students in our class.

Back in January, Heidi had mentioned that she wished her sister Evy could be her matron of honor. We called her and she was elated at the prospect so we sent her money to help with her ticket and the plan was set in motion! We also called Katie and sent her money as well because she was so happy she'd get to be there as well!

I couldn't find a dress that fit me properly and decided to make one instead. Heidi and I drove from store to store to try to find the kind of material and color she approved of. We finally found a dusty rose-colored silk that matched the color of Wylie's cummerbund of his tuxedo. I worked hard on that dress, but the silk was slippery and difficult to work with. My efforts were well rewarded though, the finished product looked lovely on my person.

Evy arrived from Sweden on August 6th. When she deplaned, tears of joy were shed by all, most of all Evy herself. Heidi drove to Portland to pick her up, then the girls stayed overnight at Heidi and Jeff's new apartment. The following day the girls drove back down to Eugene. Although Evy spoke English very well, we asked her not to strain her brain the first couple of days. While her body adjusted to the climate change, her brain needed to relax and not be forced into translating everything from Norwegian to English and back again. I promised to help her by translating as much as she wanted me to do, and so it went.

She kept pinching herself and saying that she couldn't believe that she was there. Neither could I! I put my arms around each of them and we stood there rocking to and fro quietly, taking in the moment.

"My two girls, my two girls," I said and the tears fell from all three and we knew that the moment would not happen again!

Wylie was completely taken by Evy and soon concluded that she is a very special person. For instance, the week before the wedding, Evy asked if she could clean the house for me. She wanted to do the kind of cleaning that Scandinavians do that leaves the whole house not only looking clean but smelling clean as well. I used to clean that way years ago, but my back and knees won't permit such heavy exertion.

She started washing all the curtains, windows, and walls. Then she pulled out the furniture away from the walls and wiped the walls with a damp cloth. She wouldn't let me touch a thing but only work on my dress.

Every day, Evy took a little time out to lie in the sun to get a tan. We begged her not to do it because she wasn't used to the power of the sun at this latitude. Then it happened. One evening, she got sick to her stomach. She also had a headache and a low fever and I knew she had a sunstroke. I made her take a cool bath, then sent her to bed. She slept all night and most of the following day. When she finally woke up, we reminded her how serious it could have been.

"You came very close to having a real sunstroke," I said.

"I guess I just didn't realize how strong the sun's rays are here compared to Sweden," she admitted. "I promise to listen the next time you warn me about being out in the sun." Despite her minor sunstroke, she did manage to get a nice tan while in Oregon. Katie was set to arrive on August 13th. Jeff, Heidi, Evy, and I drove to the airport to meet her noon flight. Poor Evy fought back tears and emotions that threatened to overtake her. Then the plane arrived and Katie walked in. Heidi and I stood back and let Katie and Evy have the space. Jeff stood off to the side and took pictures of the reunion between the sisters who hadn't seen each other since they were children. Evy cried and hugged Katie but Katie held her emotions in check and just smiled and held her sister. It was very odd indeed to view!

Finally, Katie greeted Heidi, Jeff and I.

After we retrieved her luggage, we piled into Jeff's car and headed back to the house. The three girls talked and talked all the way home. I fixed lunch for all of us, and then we sat and talked and just enjoyed each other's company.

The following day was Friday and Wylie and I decided to do some shopping since we wouldn't be going on Saturday, because of the wedding. Katie and Evy came along but Heidi stayed home to try to catch up on sleep. On the way home we stopped for coffee and doughnuts. When we came home, we found my father-in-law waiting outside the door. He had just arrived by train from CA.

"I forgot to call you before I left Davis," he explained. "I tried to call you when I arrived here but no answer so I took a taxi!"

It was a happy reunion among family members and Evy fit right in.

"I feel as if I have finally come home," she told me later.

The night before the wedding the three girls went out on the town while Wylie and I caught our breaths at home with my father-in-law. Gary, a friend of Jeff's, came and brought Jeff to his house to spend the night.

The girls pulled in around 2;30 AM, somewhat inebriated, so they went straight to bed. When the alarm rang at 6;30 AM, I jumped out of bed. I knew everybody was counting on me to hold this day together. I dressed quickly and went to wake the girls. Evy, Heidi, and I had appointments at the hairdresser at 8 AM.

Katie didn't want anybody to fuss with her hair other than her hairdresser in CA, so she went back to sleep. Evy sat at the breakfast table with Wylie and me. I pleaded with Heidi, who had also sat down and poured herself a cup of coffee. I pleaded again and Heidi had toast with cheese.

When we arrived at the hairdresser, no one was there yet. Finally, the beautician arrived. Rose was a 'talker' who became involved in conversations while she worked.

Sometimes she forgot and at one point, I had to remind her that time was running short and we had to be back at the house at ten o'clock for pictures! When beautician no.2 arrived, Rose said she did not need assistance and would not let her help. She finally finished at 9;45 and we dashed home!

Chapter 12

When we walked in, the house was already full of people. I greeted a few, then I ran upstairs to change clothes. I helped Heidi with her dress and then finished getting ready. My new, silky dress and new shoes made me feel so luxurious. I even managed to put on decent-looking make-up! The girls and I took turns in front of the mirror, applying our makeup was hectic but oh so much fun! Out of earshot of the rest of the people, Evy whispered:" I never thought I would live to see my mother giggling and applying make-up along with me and my sisters," and gave me a quick hug. She looked Heavenly pretty in her white dress with a wide pink belt and white high-heeled shoes. She also wore a pearl necklace and matching earrings.

Katie also wore pearls and a blue dress that echoed her beautiful blue eyes and she had her hair tinted a lovely copper shade for the wedding.

Heidi was a vision of loveliness! Her gown was white with a four-foot train and a high neckline. Instead of a veil. She had a spray of flowers in her hair. Jeff put a sixpence coin in her shoe. For something blue, she wore my Sapphire ring and something borrowed, my brooch from Norway, which my great-grandfather made for my grandmother in his smithy shop!

The photographer was nearly finished taking pictures when the limousine arrived to drive the female half of the wedding party at the rose garden, where the ceremony was to be held. I was glad to see the chairs had arrived because most of the guests were already there. The photographer milled around for candid shots. Then the crew from the local TV station arrived to interview the girls about their reunion. I called the station and asked if they would like to run their story. The program director thought it would be a nice 'human interest' feature to run. When the interview was over, the ceremony started.

A couple Kenny and Mira, provided the music were friends of Jeff and very good at what they did.

A 'hush' went over the crowd as Kenny and Mira started to sing an old Beatles tune, 'Here- There -and Everywhere.'

Up the aisle came Wylie, all smiles- in his gray tuxedo, escorting Heidi to her future husband – and her future life. She looked so lovely in her gown. The glow of her smile and the natural blush in her cheeks competed with the reds in the roses of her bouquet. Wylie delivered her at Jeff's side, then he waited until the minister motioned him to sit down by my side. I took his hand, and it felt cold and clammy. I gave the hand a squeeze and he squeezed back hard.

During the ceremony, I watched Evy and Katie, most of the time Katie had a little smile on her face but not Evy. She was so nervous and the bouquet that she was holding shook so hard that it looked as if an earthquake had hit the spot where she was standing. Her face gradually became more and more red while she was fighting back tears. Later she shared with me what she had been thinking about." At first, she thought about her own broken marriage, then thoughts about how lovely this ceremony was to her and how happy the bride and groom looked. But most of all, I couldn't stop thinking about how unbelievable it was to be standing on American soil among my 'real' family and new friends. I felt like a ship that had been lost at sea and suddenly found the old safe harbor that it had been searching for all these years".

The ceremony lasted 25 minutes. The bride and groom exchanged vows which Jeff had written and was very lovely. After the minister introduced Mr. and MRS. Reece, Jeff, and Heidi came down the aisle to the music of 'When I'm Sixty ' from the Beatles' Sargent Pepper's Lonely Hearts Club album. It was fun with a change of pace from the usual ceremonious music played at weddings, and it fit right in with the garden atmosphere.

The rose garden was in full bloom and the heavy fragrance of the flowers wafted through the air. The ceremony was held 70 yards away from the freeway overpass and every other car that drove past the garden saw what was going on and honked. After the ceremony was done, came the congratulations with hugs, kisses, and tears. While the photographer took candid shots of the bride and groom, some of the guests began to head back to the house for the reception. The bride and groom and Lizzi, rode back in the limo, while Katie, Evy, and I rode back with Wylie. It was a quiet drive because we all were busy with our own thoughts. When someone spoke, it was about the ceremony. When we arrived home, the cars were parked all around the cul-de-sac and in our driveway and Wylie had to park across the street. Our house was full of people! I felt a bit sorry for Jim (the chef). He was still working hard on the final preparations. He did have two women helping him through though, he worked the way I do, HARD and INTENSE, and had as much trouble delegating work as I do. As soon as we walked into the house, Wylie disappeared and a while later, he came down wearing slacks and a shirt so I guessed he felt uncomfortable in the tuxedo.

Wylie was running here and there, doing things that others could have done but I think he felt much too nervous to sit still and felt he had to do something. It bothered me a bit that I couldn't catch up with him, but I understood how he felt.

Katie and Evy also changed clothes. Jeff and Heidi appeared, I think they had been in one of the rooms upstairs, to grab a few moments alone before the big finale of the day arrived. They had also worked with Pastor Miller in filling out their marriage certificate, while I wrote a check for the pastor for his services. I had known Pastor Miller for many years through the church where I sang in the choir. Heidi liked his views and he was young so she wanted him to perform the service.

Jeff met the pastor and liked him right away. After they signed the papers, it was time for the champagne. Everyone went out to the garden and toasted the couple on their special day as the photographer snapped candid shots.

The food was brought out, I thought Jim had done an excellent job!

There were salads, fruits, cheeses, meats, rolls, breads, along with fruit punch and champagne punch. When most of the people were finished eating, Jeff and Heidi cut the lovely three-tiered wedding cake, which had ivory frosting with lavender and pink flowers spiraling to the top, where two glass swans sat forming a heart with their graceful necks. The presents were opened and Darla, a friend of mine, wrote down what they received and from whom. The dancing had begun and Gary's three boys (ages 9-11) kept busy dancing with the women they dared to ask- Evy, Katie, Heidi and I, all had out turn dancing. It was getting dark, people began to leave, especially those who had a longer way to drive. The wedding and reception had gone off without a hitch, except for one very sad detail- NO ONE from Jeff's family had been there! I could tell that he had a difficult time dealing with that and accepting it so Wylie and I did what we could to close his confusion.

By nine o'clock, the food and tables had been removed from the lawn. The food was placed on the kitchen table along with what was left of the cake, except for the cake top, which was wrapped in saran wrap and placed in the freezer. At dusk, Evy and I decided that the groom and bride should spend the wedding night away from the house called a motel and reserved the bridal suite. Evy and I drove to the motel and decorated the room with leftover crepe paper. We then short-changed the bed and decorated the door.

When we came back to the house, the champagne was still flowing and everyone was having a seemingly good time! It got dark and Kathy and Gary and their three sons were the only ones left. Evy made me aware of the boys acting odd and she started watching them soon she discovered that they were helping themselves to the champagne punch and had become inebriated so she talked to the parents and they were surprised at that and thought they'd better take them home and let them sleep it off! The boys loved Heidi because she had been a 'regular' at their house for a long time because… For many years, Kathy had been like a 'big sister' to Heidi because at one time Heidi was going through a difficult time in her life while she was attending high school and started confiding in Kathy because she felt that she couldn't speak with me and that it was easier to speak with someone outside of the family. At first, I truly resented that she spoke with 'this woman' but after a while, I got used to the idea. She apparently needed to speak with someone who was not family, I deduced. Maybe this woman will 'set her straight'!

Kathy did just that! She helped Heidi see things from a different approach. Heidi never told me what they talked about. Sometimes when she came from Kathy's house she would be bursting at the seams with happiness and would give me highlights from their talk. Once she seemed uncomfortable about telling me what they had discussed.

"You know dear, you don't have to feel obligated to tell me anything you two talked about," I said. "To tell you the truth, I'd rather not know, it's between Kathy and yourself."

She looked searchingly at my face for a moment, then looked down at her hands and her face turned red and she smiled bashfully. The silence was deafening until for some dumb reason I stretched and burped.

Usually, Heidi hated it when anyone burped without excusing themselves, but this time we just looked at each other and burst into laughter, a true tension release.

But back to the evening of the wedding….

Kathy wanted to know if anything had been done to Jeff's car….

No one had even thought of it!

"Well, we have to do something," she said in a devilish voice.

I warned her that Heidi had just had it painted two days before the wedding so whatever we did, had to be done carefully. Kathy took a deep red lipstick and wrote on all the windows things like; I love you, forever love, etc. Then we decorated the car with crepe paper on the inside and the final touch was Kathy's idea with crumpled paper bags on all the seats. At about 10:30 Heidi and Jeff thought they'd better get some sleep, and we all followed them out to see them off and threw birdseed. Heidi and Jeff left, followed by Kathy and Gary and the boys, and lastly the musicians. Then Wylie's dad went to bed and that left Evy, Katie, Wylie, and I. I looked at Evy and she looked as if she was ready for bed she said 'good night' and went to bed as well. I thought she went to bed because had so little sleep the night before but she told me later that she went to bed partly because of the way Katie carried on. That was true, Katie didn't want to stop partying. The rest of us were ready to fall into bed but she wanted to continue drinking. Wylie didn't want to be rude and leave her there all alone and sat with her for a while. After I went to bed, Katie came upstairs to give me a hug and say 'good night'. She started talking about personal 'things' and ended up crying in my arms. It bothers me a lot that she becomes vulnerable only when she is drinking. Then she is very tender and open with her thoughts.

Throughout the wedding day, she had called me 'mama' and it made me feel warm and fulfilled even though I knew it was just a 'put on' since Evy and Heidi called me that. Katie probably thought people would wonder why she didn't, especially since all of them knew that she was my daughter.

The following morning, I woke up earlier than usual to tackle the kitchen which was covered with dirty dishes everywhere. Since I didn't have a dishwasher, it was up to me to clean them. I fed the dog and cat, had a little breakfast, then made coffee for the rest of the 'gang', before I started my chores.

Soon Wylie's dad came down, followed by Wylie, Evy, and lastly Katie. They all had breakfast except Katie, she downed cup after cup of coffee, I never saw her eat breakfast! And then it was back to straightening up the house again! Evy grabbed the mop and bucket and started on the floors! Katie didn't do much of anything except walk around talking -mostly to Dad and that was a good thing! Wylie went out in the yard to finish the clean-up out there and Katie followed him.

Close to lunchtime, Heidi and Jeff returned from the motel, happy and hungry. The girls helped me fix lunch, and then we all ate and talked about the wedding day.

Then Heidi and Jeff wanted to get going on the drive to Portland since he had to work the next day. Wylie and the girls helped load their presents into the van and they were off.

Evy grabbed the mop and bucket and started upstairs, all the while Katie stayed out of the way. We had so much food left that there wasn't room in the fridge or freezer, so I gave some to the man who lived across the street, who accepted it gladly!

Katie left on Tuesday. Since Wylie had gone back to work, Dad, Evy, and I drove her to the airport. Katie liked Dad and thought it was nice to have a new grandpa. Dad had become fond of her as well. We all said our 'goodbye', then the plane left.

After Katie had gone, Evy cried and cried as she asked, "Why doesn't Katie return my sister's love for her?"

"She will, in time," I assured her. "Right now, she's probably quite overwhelmed with what she has been through while she was with us!" Evy seemed to accept it.

Evy and I drove Dad to the railroad station the following day. It was another sad 'goodbye' for Evy and she cried all the way home.

"I finally have found a real grandpa and I had to say 'good-bye' to him," she said sadly, shaking her head as she searched her purse for a Kleenex.

With Wylie working and everyone else gone, the house had once again become quiet and peaceful. Evy and I had a chance to do a lot of talking.

One evening we sat in our garden with our coffee and the conversation led to her childhood and she became thoughtful for a moment.

"You know mama, I hated you for not trying to bring me to the USA to live with you and Wylie! Why didn't you try?" she wanted to know.

I must have looked absolutely dumbfounded for an instant....

"But I did!" I said." I tried when you were ten years old. Wylie and I wrote to Mama and said we would like to have you here with us. She wrote back and said you had a lot of medical problems, mostly with your eyes. You were having blackouts and headaches and they were going to bring you to a specialist to find out if there was a possibility of a tumor. For that reason, you would have to stay there, so there was no reason to talk about it anymore."

She wiped the tears from her eyes and continued, "I used to feel so sad because I thought you didn't want me and I hated you for it. When I tried to talk with Grandma about it, she'd say," Aren't you glad you're here with us? But I always felt there was something missing from my life. I never knew what it was until now. I was missing you!! Since I've been in America, I've felt as if I've come home, I have been mended and am whole again. But no matter how hard I try to describe this wonderful feeling; the words just won't come forth!"

Evy and I talked and talked and the days flew by. The week-end before she was to fly back to Sweden, Wylie, Evy and I drove up to the famous lava beds of Oregon.

She was in awe at the breathtaking sites. She took lots of pictures of those lovely scenes. Sometimes, she got nervous at some of the places we took her to because of her fear of heights. We tried to reassure her and let her go at her own pace. When driving back to town, I thought I could detect a note of pride in her voice. She had actually walked to the edge of a cliff and looked at the road below! Even though she held onto Wylie the whole time, it was still a big accomplishment and thrill for her and we congratulated her on her achievement!

During the last two days of her visit, she shopped for clothes and toys for the children.

On August the 23rd 1987, Wylie and I drove her to Portland, where we all would stay overnight at Jeff and Heidi's apartment. Her plane was leaving the following morning at 7 AM. It was a hot and depressing evening and I don't think any of us got any sleep. The following morning, we were all up at 5;30 AM. Heidi made coffee and we all had a small breakfast because we planned on going out for breakfast after Evy's departure.

We all said our tearful 'goodbyes', even Wylie was moved. He has fully accepted her as his daughter!

"Why do I always say 'goodbye' to the ones I love?" Evy asked Wylie tearfully as she had her arms around him.

Because of mechanical failure, the plane was delayed 30 minutes, which stretched to 45min. All the passengers sat on the plane and waited, a nerve-racking experience, I know from my own travels.

After the plane finally took off, the four of us walked back to the car and out to breakfast we headed. Our table was quiet as we had our own thoughts. Heidi had said that Jeff really liked Evy and was looking forward to having her as his sister-in-law. At the time, Jeff collected teddy bears of all kinds. He gave Evy his most prized bear as a 'going away' present! Heidi said she was surprised at his gesture, but she said he would do anything for someone he liked a lot. She says she gets so tickled at the way he talks about visiting Evy in Sweden someday!

Our routines had mostly settled back down to normal, whatever that may be.

My orthopedic doctor checked my knee and then sent me to the Injured Workers Program to see if I could possibly enter the workforce again. The therapists ran tests on my knee, then asked, if possible, it may be a good idea if I tried to lose 20 lbs. before I re-enter the program. My knees are weak and definitely need special care and training and my back also needs help.

So far, I have lost 13 lbs. and feel good about myself. I'm on a long-term weight loss program. Since I didn't gain this weight quickly, it won't come off quickly!

I'm not on a 'true' diet, but a program I found in a magazine that sounded so reasonable and easy to handle, and thought I'd give it a try. For self-help, I meditate and ask a 'higher power 'to release me from this jail of fat. Once per week, I go off my program and eat what I want, including desserts. It relaxes me and helps me keep on my program. I don't look at it as cheating but rather as another form of self-help.

As far as I am concerned, being overweight is a chemical imbalance of the mind in which heredity plays a major part. But for me and my body, losing weight quickly is not the answer- so I'm taking it slow and easy and it's going well.

Soon Wylie and I will be grandparents again! Heidi is expecting a baby toward the end of February. This will be his first maternal grandchild. The impact hasn't hit him yet and probably won't until he holds the baby for the first time.

I'm very satisfied with life now. I have a husband and children who love me and whom I love in return. I have found a job and now the second part of my life will begin. But still, I wanted more from this- my life. The job I HAD did not satisfy -and for a while, I went from job to job and Wylie began to wonder as did I. But he began to question the situation and that made me feel inadequate, sad, and irritated at the world! I wanted my own little restaurant!! There- I said that thought out aloud! Now I knew what I had wanted all along! With that 'fire in my belly, I started working on my project by putting menus together and food tastes from the 5 Scandinavian Countries. The only country I didn't have any recipes from was Iceland. Week after week I poured through libraries until I finally found one address in New York. I wrote a query letter to the address and it had been forwarded to an Icelandic chef in New York -who took the time to gather and send a very large number of recipes for which I was elated. I sent him a 'thank you' note to thank him for his kindness. Finally, my menu was ready and now I could concentrate on the final step in my journey- the financing!

My friend – who was to be my partner on my side journeyed from one business to the next, trying to open doors! I found a 1960s two-story house in the small town next to our town and fell in love with the house. Wylie and I looked at it first, then I brought my friend there and he thought it would be perfect for our venture. We worked out the math and figured we would need around $75,000 to get started. We scraped our savings together and found we had only $25,000- the rest we had to find somewhere! But where? We tried the banks but they charged too much interest. My friend and I agonized for a while but- finally, we HAD TO face the facts-- This just wasn't going to work at all! After all that work, we put it into!!

After I put all the plans and menus away and bid on the house, I sank into depression and felt that I had failed in life as a businesswoman! My husband didn't have much to say on the matter at hand as he had never given any verbal support at any time that I could recall. Instead, I went to the Small Business office and spoke with a man who became my mentor, and he suggested that I take the 'wait and see' attitude. He looked at all my preparations and said that I had done an excellent job. However, the economy was slow and business was playing a 'wait' see' game. So, it was- and I finally understood that it was not ME!

In my own way of looking at it, thought that the World was not ready to meet me and my venture so I tabled my dream and went to work cooking at restaurants!

My husband was never satisfied with my job at any time! I would come home from work, dig right in and make dinner, take care of the house, make his lunches, and prepare for the next day.

He had become sullen and had started drinking a bit more than before and wouldn't talk to me about what was the matter. He drew more and more away from me and I hoped it wasn't another woman – I couldn't figure it out!

At this time Heidi called and said that she and her little family were moving back to Eugene or nearby and I was elated! She said she wanted to become a nurse and would enroll in school, which she did and graduated as an LPN and went to work right away to try out her new journey! I thought they were happy now that she had a job but they were not! Jeff was extremely jealous of Heidi's personal friends, whom she had hung out with since childhood and whom he had known about since they first met. He had tried to talk to her about letting go of these friends, claiming she had enough friendship in him but she said she needed her friends and he got angry. This she related to me, as she cried bitterly. He also didn't want her to work because he worked and she should stay home with their child!

Anyway, it ended in divorce! The agreement was that Jeff would keep the son Tristan and she said;" I can always have more babies". She packed her things and moved to Davis CA and got a job in Sacramento at the airport as a ticket agent to which she had gone to school in Florida, so she was certified. After her move, I missed her an awful lot and we spoke on the phone as often as we could. Since her little family was 'broken,' we did as much as humanly possible for our grandson. We offered to bring the boy to Eugene and raise him and that his father could have him on visits, any time he wanted. There came an absolute "NO" and backed it up with that "he wouldn't be a good and proper father if he agreed to that"! Wylie and I were in shock at his decision. Heidi called and said she missed the boy so much and wondered if we could bring him down to her for a visit. Wylie couldn't take off from work but I could go. I arranged with Jeff to pick the boy up at his home and the following AM I picked him up and drove to Davis, CA, a 7 HR drive! Heidi was elated to be seeing her son and when I saw the bond between those two, my heart ached at the thought of separating them again! All too soon, the week came to an end and we had to leave and mother and son said a tearful 'goodbye'. All the way up toward home, Tristan was quiet and I knew where his thoughts were and left him alone. I dropped him off at his house, which was empty and his father wouldn't be home until later. I felt very uneasy leaving him in the empty house in the state of mind he was in. I would much rather have brought him home with me but I knew Jeff would not have allowed that at all! A few weeks later Heidi called and said that she was moving back to Oregon and she had been transferred to Portland Airport, I was beyond happy! When she arrived, she stayed with us for a week then on to Portland where she secured herself an apartment. We didn't hear from her for a couple of weeks, then I called her. She said she was alright but not much money. After that, I made it a point to call her once a week and she wouldn't have to spend her money on the phone call. Heidi talked to Tristan and he told her that his father had a new girlfriend but Tristan didn't like her that much. I assured her as best I could that all was alright. At that time, Wylie's aunt and uncle from Davis had moved to Salem here in Oregon and built a lovely home. They invited Wylie, Heidi, and myself to come and visit. When Heidi arrived, my jaw dropped at the sight of her! She must have lost at least 40 lbs. since we saw her last! I asked gently what was going on. She was embarrassed as she said;" You see mama, by the time I've paid all my bills, there's not much money left for food!" I was shocked and asked, "Then what will you do next?" She looked down at her hands in her lap as she answered, "I think I'll be moving back to Eugene." That was the best news I'd ever had! Wylie co-signed on a little house for her and she moved in with a girlfriend, to help share the expenses but the girlfriend's two kids moved in as well! Heidi got a boyfriend and a very good office job with an electric company and she was beyond happy. Then Jeff called and said that he was signing Tristan over to her permanently and she, in turn, told us the good news! The news came in January and when the school year ended in June, Tristan would make the move. I had lunch with her a week or so later and noticed her constantly playing with a small lump that sat supported on the front of her collarbone. I asked what that was but she didn't know and said she didn't have insurance so she could not see the doctor. I went cold all over with worry.

I suggested that she should go to visit our doctor under our plan.

The doctor examined her and immediately sent her to see a specialist who operated and discovered cancer! She underwent chemo and took medications that bloated her terribly and she lost all of her beautiful hair.

One day, she asked me to come and have lunch with her. I made our lunch and coffee.

After she ate, she made a bathroom stop. While in there, she called out to me to come into the bathroom and saw the toilet bowl filled with blood and she said;" mama, we need to go to the emergency room -NOW!

I glanced at her and I suddenly felt oddly calm. I checked the coffee pot, it was turned off, I grabbed my purse and found her waiting for me in the car. I drove to the hospital's emergency entrance and she walked calmly in and the nurses took her through the doors right away. I don't know how long I waited because everything was in a blur. Then the attending nurse asked me to come in the back and I was ushered to a private room where she told me that Heidi had passed away!

I felt as if I had fallen into an icy cold crevasse with no way of getting out! I couldn't move and felt as if I couldn't breathe either. I tried to breathe but to no avail. I heard the nurse's command far, far away as she pulled at my arm saying, "Sit down, sit down!" Then from somewhere, I heard a scream- then I surfaced as I felt tears running down my cheeks as I was screaming; "NO, NO- it isn't true!" She quietly left the room and came back with a glass of cold water and ordered me to drink some and I obeyed. Then she asked if I had driven us to the hospital- I finally was able to somewhat focus and answered that I had driven. She then asked if I had somebody that needed to be contacted. Now I could fully control my mind and answered; "Yes, my husband. I started dialing, the phone rang and Wylie answered and I told him and he said that he was on his way but he had to take the bus, so it would be a while before getting to the hospital! I finally 'crawled out of my proverbial crevasse' and felt calm and collected but I caught myself studying the wall clock, noticing the hands moved extremely slowly for some odd reason and I couldn't figure that out! The nurse came and asked me to follow her to another room, where they had placed the naked body of my girl on a table with a blanket covering him. I stood there waiting for her to open her beautiful brown eyes, look at me, and say:" April fool!" It didn't happen!

The door opened and Wylie walked in. I ran to him to be held and be close to him.

We stood holding on to each other closely. I noticed that he just stood there very rigidly and didn't cry at all that I could see. I thought it was very odd but didn't say anything because I knew he was grieving in his own way. This was his only child and he didn't get to keep her with him on earth.

The nurse came in with a request; A young girl from Portland needed eyes, might we give our consent in the donation of Heidi's eyes… Wylie and I looked at each other and he said;" Why not, she was a nurse that hoped to save lives, so why not?" Right away two ice bags were placed on Heidi's eyes to preserve them and later that day, the eyes would be express-driven to Portland! We finally said 'goodbye' and Wylie drove us home. I had nothing planned for our dinner, and we had sandwiches but neither of us ate but a couple of bites. We went to bed but we tossed and turned most of the night. Then we started talking and made small talk the rest of the night. We did not speak of our girl, that was too painful, like an open wound.

Wylie played the bagpipes every day all the while walking back and forth in our backyard. One day I asked him about a tune I didn't recognize and which he played every day. His eyes were red and I knew he had been crying. He looked at the pipes and said;" This piece of music came through the pipe and I HAVE TO play it every time I have the pipe in my hands!" "It's lovely," I said," and must be recorded!"

"The only trouble is that it sounds different every time I play it!"

"Still," I said-" you must record it or write the music down for others to enjoy."

At the memorial, he stood up and played that piece of music in front of the audience. When he finished and sat down, he cried and at that moment I thought he had come full circle in his grief! Little did I know that was not the case. We were all sitting with our own thoughts when suddenly a child started crying, almost screaming out loud- Tristan who sat next to his father stood up and ran and buried his face in Wylie's chest while sobbing and saying;" Mama, mama, come back to me – I love you!" Wylie held him tight until his cry stopped and his father just sat there stone-faced staring straight ahead and I thought 'How can you just sit there and not console your son! Damn you!'

I felt full of anger but I guess Heidi pulled me back because the thoughts left as quickly as they came! After a while, Tristan's cries quieted and he sat down next to Wylie, holding onto his arm and leaning his head on Wylie's shoulder. In my sorrow, I discovered all was silent in the room. David, Heidi's very best friend all through the school years and her adult life was in charge of the music. He was crying and the music had stopped. Our friends were all shedding tears and all the while watching Tristan and some were shaking their heads and I am certain that I knew from what!! After the memorial, there were no refreshments as I had no one helping me with this task. Jeff turned to Tristan and said;" Well Tristan, mama is gone and now you and I have to go on." I was speechless as I looked at Wylie who had a blank look on his face. Tristan ran to Wylie and held tight as he said; "I want to stay for a while!" I suggested letting the boy stay for the week-end but Jeff said a flat 'NO!' My heart ached and cried for the boy and at what Jeff couldn't or wouldn't see, how his sweet son was suffering. Heidi's wish was to be cremated and we fulfilled her wish and placed her urn on our mantle. The following summer Evy was planning on coming and bringing her 3 children, a boy (16), and twin girls (19) to visit. I was emerging from the grief haze and had started thinking clearer, and I asked Wylie if he still was entertaining the idea of adopting Evy. A little smile came to his lips as he said;" As a matter of fact I am!" We started the paperwork and through our attorney as well as Wylie himself, we found out that we needed her real birth certificate. I called her and stated what I wanted. She became very suspicious and started asking questions so I made up a story of having to prove she was Heidi's sister, anyway- she believed me finally. We started looking forward to them coming. We called Jeff's house every week to find out how Tristan was doing and all we heard was; "He's doing alright". Then one day, I got a call from his school asking what was going on in his life. Saying that his grades had gone from top grades to below the lowest!

He was pulling all kinds of jokes on kids he didn't like and had come to the point of possibly being expelled from school. I was horrified and asked if his father had informed the school what had happened. She said that the school knew nothing and I was speechless at the thought that Jeff had not informed the school as to what had transpired in the boy's life! I then asked for a meeting with all his teachers and the school counselor and suggested not letting the boy know we were there until the meeting was done and school was out for the day. The meeting went well until I requested for Tristan to be counseled once per week and the counselor replied 'that he didn't know if he could do that as he wore many hats!' and was very busy! I became very upset and asked if he realized the trauma the boy had been through! He squirmed as the principal said;" Tristan will have a counseling session once a week for a while forward!" I calmed down as I answered that I would call to check if he had his counseling but I didn't say who I would be calling. The meeting adjourned and I asked to let Tristan know we were at school to visit with him. He came running out the door and into our arms. We knew he hadn't had a bath in many days because of his body odor. We asked about that ever so carefully and he said that there was something wrong with the water flow to the tub. Wylie and I agreed that Jeff must be showering at work and that made me very upset! While we were there, Jeff arrived saying he had worked overtime and had to go to bed right away! He never asked the boy about his day or any of that sort! We chatted with Tristan for a while and carefully led the conversation to his school. He wanted to know why Wylie and I were at the school and we said it was to find out why he was in trouble and asked if he would like to share with us why...We assured him that we were not angry with him, just puzzled. He looked down as he began talking. There was this boy who was always teasing him for not having a mother. Wylie and I exchanged glances as I asked if he had shared this with the counselor.

Chapter 13

He looked at each of us as he said that he hadn't seen the counselor in two weeks! The day after we had seen Tristan, I called the school and spoke with the principal as well as the counselor asking why the boy hadn't had a session in two weeks. The counselor said he had been busy and once again said 'that he wore many hats!' I said that I knew but I was looking out for the boy's mental well-being and suggested that if it was more important for him to be 'doing other things' than to help a child find solutions to his sorrow and loss of a parent, he might as well throw his counseling hat in the trash, it's not worth a plug penny!

The principal must have been listening in, because she asked me not to be so 'harsh!' I asked if she had children and she said 'yes'. I asked if she had had a child die. 'No' she answered. "Then how can you possibly ask me not to feel this way?" I asked, and I felt my throat tightening with anger and frustration. I said that I had to hang up the phone before I said something I'd regret later but before I did, I made the counselor promise me that he would help the boy find clarity by having a session per week until the end of the school year and he promised he would. I called Tristan several times per week and asked casually – and the answer was always 'yes', he had sessions every week! When school was out, Wylie and I drove to their home and said to Jeff it might be a good idea to 'give him Jeff, a 'breather' by letting the boy spend the summer with us, and with Jeff's given permission, we'd enroll him in 'grief camp', to which he reluctantly agreed, although he didn't think the boy needed this camp!! We enrolled Tristan for

175

which Wylie and I paid and I drove him there. When we picked him up, one of the counselors spoke with us about how great it was to see how Tristan acted between the other children and their grief! Then he asked, if at all possible, could Tristan come back the following summer to assist with some children. Both Wylie and I said that we'd try to make it happen by asking his father's permission. The counselor went on to say that the camp fee would be very small. They had watched Tristan and were amazed at how easily he got 'through' to some of the kids who had problems opening up to the counselors but did to him. Because he would tell them how he felt and they, in turn, would speak about their feelings.

On the way back from camp, Tristan told of all the things he had done and of some of the kids and their grieving. He wrote a poem about his grief and this poem was read at a radio station in Seattle!

The following summer Jeff allowed Tristan to spend the summer with us and also go to camp and I was on the 7th Cloud of Happiness!! Then Evy called and said that she and the kids would like to come and spend some time with us, to which Wylie and I both agreed. After I hung up the phone, I started wondering HOW would we keep our sanity with 3 teenagers of various ages, in the house at the same time. Oh Yes- We found out later! We started making plans as to where to take them and what to see. We had so many places in this state to see. Since Tristan had not had any siblings- and when arguments broke out, he'd be confused! It happened and he went to Evy and asked for an explanation as to why they behaved like that. Evy said that this is what they did for 'blowing off steam' several times a week because twins think alike much of the time and when they argued, little brother stayed out of the way until they were done. Dan tried to explain to Tristan what was happening and I guess Tristan accepted his answer. The following morning the girls were planning on going to the lake to tan but Wylie and I said; "No" that we had something to do that involved the whole family! They wanted to know but we said it was a secret and then we suggested that they dress nicely! Evy said that we should tell her at least but we said 'no' to that as well!

We drove up in front of the attorney's office and were ushered right in. The man shook our hands and asked Evy and Wylie to sit up front, closest to his desk. He explained to Evy what was about to happen and from her facial expression, I saw that she was taken totally by surprise. So much in fact, that she forgot her English and spoke Norwegian instead! That broke the tension in the room and we burst out in laughter! After Wylie was sworn in as father and his promise made, Evy stood up from her chair and wrapped her arms around him and tearfully said that this was what she had been wishing for a long time and now it had come true!!

We celebrated by going out to dinner but when we came home, the twins started pouting because they didn't get to go tanning! Dan diplomatically answered that what had happened was more important and a lot more fun than tanning. Tristan nodded in agreement and the girls were quiet.

The kids retired for the evening and Evy, Wylie, and I had coffee. She sat her cup down and while her tears were flowing said," Now my life's complete- I got a father- a dad who loves me for who I am!"

I glanced at Wylie, and he was grinning from ear to ear and my heart sang! I think in part- this episode helped heal me and the deep sorrow I carry in my heart- less painful! The rest of Evy's stay was busy with the kids' demands, which left Tristan very confused. One day, he came to me shaking his head saying; "You know, Grandma, I'm really glad I'm an only child, this way I don't have to fight with somebody all the time!" I was really surprised by his comments. I said; "They don't argue ALL the time and they are twins and they do think alike! Then little brother steps in the middle -but- the main thing is that they love each other and that there's a lot of respect for each other as well!" He thought for a moment then he said quietly; "I guess you are right, Grandma because that's what Dan said also" but he added, "It still scares me!"

The day of Heidi's inurnment was bright and sunny. Evy was seemingly nervous because she had not seen this performed before. Beforehand, I had explained to her what was to happen. She readied her kids. Tristan donned his kilt as did Wylie for he was to play his bagpipes for Heidi.

We were all quiet and thinking our own thoughts while driving to the site.

A friend of mine who sang professionally would sing a couple of hymns, which she did. Evy had lost her husband to a massive heart attack the year prior and Dan had not mourned at all, not cried nor anything else. We sat and listened to the lady sing, and then the twins started looking for their brother and saw him sitting on a bench about 20 feet from our site. The twins went to him and he was deeply crying and his sorrow had been released. We turned back to the site and discovered Tristan standing by his mom's urn and he was swaying. Wylie dropped his pipes and grabbed him just in time before he fainted and fell into the hole where the urn was to be placed and his tears were flowing as well. Wylie just held him and they both cried. The twins told Evy later that Dan had finally cried, she smiled and said; "Now the healing begins for my boy!" Later we joined the singer at a little restaurant for a somber but enjoyable lunch.

After Evy and the kids went back to Sweden, Tristan had his final week at camp, where he helped counsel some of the kids. After the completion of the camp, he was very excited while saying 'goodbye' to all his newfound friends, and on the way home to our house, he said in his quiet way;" I want to do this next summer as well!" At that moment, I felt very proud of my precious grandson and wished I would stand by this young lad through life or as long as I lived!

After Evy and the kids left for Sweden, Wylie and I were exhausted and Tristan became his quiet self again. Sometimes he would ask questions about his cousins and Wylie and I would try to give him the answer we hoped would satisfy. Sometimes it worked and other times it didn't. Then came time for our little boy to go back to his dad and continue school. The evening before we were to drive him home, he sat down next to me and leaned on my shoulder and said; "Grandma, I don't want to go home to that place. I want to stay here and go to school in Eugene!"

Wylie and I exchanged glances as Wylie suggested that he speak with his father and the principal of the school and ask for a meeting with all of us and he assured us he would do that. He began to do better in school and the 'luster' came back in his eyes and he became his sparkly old self again! With Tristan's dilemma settled, I needed something to do. Naturally, I thought of 'Baking My Great Passion' and possibly sales. I licensed my kitchen and began baking and went door to door, selling my wares but alas- there was no profit in these sales!

With the wear on the car and me- simply not profitable!

I looked toward Wylie's and mine 'great enjoyment' at the yearly Renaissance Fair.

We were recruited and helped get the first Fair on its 'feet' here in Lane County and it started in Philomath where I was the 'Village Baker' and Wylie was the 'Village Piper'. My bake shop became very popular because I took 1700-1800 yr old recipes and worked them into newer products but the ancient flavors lingered and that's why I was sought after. The 2nd yr. I sold out totally by 3 PM, drove home (1 ½ hour-drive) baked, cut wrapped, and labeled, and was back opening the next AM. We never knew if we were to sell out every year but we did this for 9 years and then we retired. It was so sad to leave this group because we knew everyone, we were like a family. Every evening, we get together and sit and talk and maybe have a drink of some kind before falling into bed from being tired. It was a lot of fun!

After retirement, I buried myself in handwork projects- specializing in knitting and 'knit for hire'. Wylie set up a 'garden railroad' in our backyard for which he was interviewed by our local newspaper. Our garden was our sanctuary where we would sit every evening with our glass of wine, then go in and have our dinner. Our cat and dog would relax with us. Our cat and dog passed away and soon we realized that the house and property were getting to be a bit too much for us to handle. We were coming on in age and it was time to sell! I cried a lot over this but it was inevitable! I had a friend who was a realtor at the fitness spa, where I had been a member for 44 years. The realtor took the job and there were only two good 'bids' and the second bid was the best one which we accepted. It was a young couple with two children that bought it. Wylie and I visited them and when we were ready to leave, the youngest of their girls latched onto me and begged me to stay saying; "please don't go but stay and be my new grandma"! The mother was so surprised, saying the girl had never done that before. I promised to come back to visit her. I visited her the second time and the girl greeted me then went on to play again. Now Wylie and I moved to Senior Living only 6 blocks from our old house. Wylie and I moved our things in just one week. For the 'heavy stuff', we paid a neighbor who moved in with his pickup and he brought his brother and they mounted our cabinet on the wall!

During the move, both Wylie and I had the flu and we were jubilating when we had all of it here and could rest which we so badly needed. This is not the end.